SEVEN MYTHS

OF SELLING TO GOVERNMENT

Secrets for Success in Government
Sales Today

Rick Wimberly & Lorin Bristow

This publication is designed to provide accurate and authoritative information in regard to the subject matter covered. It is sold with the understanding that the publisher is not engaged in rendering legal, accounting, or other professional service. If legal advice or other expert assistance is required, the services of a competent professional should be sought.

Published by Galain Publishing
106 Gillette Drive
Franklin, TN   37069

Contents

When we are no longer able to change a situation, we are challenged to change ourselves.

— Viktor Frankl

It is wiser to find out than to suppose.

— Mark Twain

People are very open-minded about new things — as long as they're exactly like the old ones.

— Charles F. Kettering

PREFACE

You're Doing it All Wrong

If you're using traditional sales techniques to sell to government, you're doing it all WRONG.

That's correct. Wrong.

This year, local, state, and federal governments will spend nearly $5 TRILLION on all sorts of things. And they will spend it with people and companies who know how to win government contracts. Will vendors win these deals because they are better at traditional selling?

Absolutely not.

Star performers in these companies know when securing lucrative government contracts, normal sales techniques simply don't work. This book will **reveal their secrets** and show you what **really drives success** in selling to local, state, and federal governments.

We will eradicate seven long-revered sales practices (plus a bonus) that are simply not effective in the government marketplace.

Learn what they are, how to change them, and what to replace them with and you'll maximize **your** success.

Five trillion dollars is a big pie (and we all love pie). Don't leave it all to the big companies. When you learn their secrets you can get a slice of it for yourself.

What is this book about?

This book is about YOU. A smart, motivated sales professional who wants to make money selling to the government.

This is not a book on how to write proposals, access contract vehicles, or find grant sources...those topics are well covered elsewhere. This *is* a book drawn from our decades of experience and success selling millions of dollars in products and services to government agencies.

We have lived what we reveal in this book, and we have stepped on more than our fair share of land mines in the process. We want to keep you from making similar mistakes while benefitting from the lessons we've learned over the years.

It's not that we didn't try traditional sales techniques.

- ✓ **We used to think RFP's drive government business.** They don't. There is something much more important and necessary.

- ✓ **We were led to believe cold-calling is king.** It isn't. But there is something that is.

- ✓ **We had been told, and believed, we should always go to the top when selling.** You shouldn't. Read the rest of this book to find out where you should go, why you should go there, and what you should do once you get there.

- ✓ **We had always believed solution selling would land the contract** until we learned why we couldn't do this even if we wanted to.

✓ **We often spent hours, even days, developing sales presentations** only to discover we were doing them all wrong. We will show you why and what you should do instead.

✓ **We developed comprehensive scripts to overcome objections and press for a close.** Then we discovered these techniques were way over-rated. Keep reading to find out which techniques really are essential.

✓ **We thought sales and marketing work hand-in-hand.** They do not. They're not even on the same planet. We will, however, reveal how to leverage the efforts of both.

✓ **And we chanted the mantra "If it is to be, it's up to me"** only to find we could not achieve the financial and personal level of success we desired all by ourselves. This book will reveal how to get it for yourself.

We will do more than uncover the practices and principles that don't work. We will open up for you a toolbox of techniques, principles, methods, systems, and attitudes that do work, and **they work unbelievably well!**

Selling to governments requires a complete package. By that we mean you need to address more than cold factual sales technique and methodology. We are confident if you understand how B2G selling is different from what you may have been taught, you, too can tap into this lucrative marketplace.

Building a Foundation

Before we delve into conquering government markets, we must first tell you a few of our biases and underlying beliefs. You'll see these woven throughout this book as they are fundamental to our approach and, we believe, your success. Warning: they can be a bit sappy, but you'll survive. Even hard-nosed sales and business development people have a few soft spots here and there (particularly the more successful ones).

Integrity

Government agencies buy products and services with taxpayers' money – OUR money. We take this seriously. Because of this, we believe a sales or business development person has a duty to provide its customers with products and services that meet the expectations they set. Keep your promises! This doesn't mean you have to give away the farm. You shouldn't. It does mean you should approach the sale with the strongest measure of ethics and honesty.

The government sales and business development secrets discussed here *will not* help you manipulate or deceive customers into buying. It *will* help you determine what really motivates customers and how to position your products and services in ways that unleash value. You'll benefit. They'll benefit.

Listening

GSS is a division of Galain Solutions, Inc. "Galain" is a Native American Indian word meaning "listen," which is something we strive to do with our customers (see how important it is?). It's also at the heart of the government selling secrets.

The harsh truth is government procurement processes often make "selling by listening" difficult to achieve. Pre-bid meetings, RFPs, contract vehicles, etc. all are designed to water down your ability to unduly influence the buyer even when intentions are otherwise honorable. There's a tremendous amount of accountability in government buying. No one, not even the President or the Mayor, really has the ability to write a check to a vendor without visibility and accountability. Not to say people haven't been caught with their hands in the government till. They have. But be assured, someone, somewhere saw them do it. In order for the government to buy something, there's generally a complex maze of things that must happen before checks are written. When you hear of abuse, it's because someone figured out how to sneak around the maze without getting caught (at least in the short term).

Unfortunately the limitations designed to protect the public's money also dilute the sincere sales professional's ability to diagnose and present creative solutions. Despite the challenge, this book will teach you ways for getting to the heart of buyers' needs, then presenting your approach to fixing the problem – despite the maze you'll be navigating.

Process

While we are not big fans of imposing weighty, rigid processes on sales teams, we have observed and fostered over the years certain consistent behaviors of top producers. Successful sales and business development people appreciate good processes. They embrace them. Weak performers hate them. (Umm, it is the processes they hate, not necessarily their successful colleagues…well, most of the time, anyway).

We believe outlining and distilling these habits (many of them natural tendencies) into a replicable, teachable process can positively impact individual results. We've seen it first-hand. So, we offer this sales model as a guideline for success – not something to focus on with such intensity it becomes its own distraction.

By dispelling the myths and practicing the secrets presented here, you can thrive in government sales, creating a lucrative long-term income stream that compounds year by year.

Patience

We're going to show you short-cuts, but they may not be what you would think. Our short-cuts come from placing you on a path, showing you how to navigate it, and encouraging you to stay on the path – even though the path is a not a short one. Government sales cycles are long…real long. Pretty much everyone knows that, but often we see people lulled into a belief they're going to get lucky and huge government orders are going to fall from the sky in short order. They say they know better, but when a year passes and government sales haven't closed, they start looking toward the blue sky. When they see nothing but blinding light, they lose patience and get off the path on which they embarked.

Don't get us wrong. Even the best of paths need navigational adjustments. But getting too far off the path means you just waste time trying to find your way back. This is a common problem in government sales. We've seen it time and time again.

However, there are good maps (or I guess we should say good GPS devices) available. And, the rewards for staying the course can be quite nice indeed.

Are you ready to open your mind to new ideas that may challenge your old ways of thinking? Are you prepared to eradicate harmful selling myths and succeed like never before in government sales? Then read on and let our odyssey begin.

CHAPTER ONE

MYTH #1: RFPs drive government business.

FACT #1: Relationships drive government business.

When we first talk with potential clients who have little or no experience in the government space, they usually tell us their approach to government business has but two tracks - go to some trade shows and respond to some RFPs. They want us to tell them which shows to attend and, even more importantly, show them how to uncover more RFPs.

Ah, if it were only that easy! Business owners hear about people getting rich selling to the government. They hear about the huge amounts of money the government is spending in an effort to sweeten the economy. Their attention is captured by ads in magazines, even infomercials on TV, about how easy it can be to sell to the government. They want in on the action, too, and think all they have to do is respond to some RFPs. Even experienced government business bosses think RFP responses is how they're making money. They are wrong!

We work with a client who, for more than thirty years, has an impressive record of winning RFPs. Their win rate is well over 80%. Meantime, we know another company with a win rate of less than 10%. Both bid on $100,000-plus solution-oriented contracts. Both have strong credentials and impressive stories to tell. Both are priced competitively.

Here's where they are different: the winning company will not submit a response to an RFP, even if well-qualified for the opportunity, unless they have an established relationship and have been involved well before the RFP was issued. The losing company will bid on virtually any opportunity where they could possibly meet the specifications, prior established relationship or not.

You can imagine the difference in efficiency and effectiveness between these two companies. Enormous amounts of time and energy are expended in the RFP-oriented company. Lead generation, relationship building, and product development suffer because everyone is too "busy". After all, an approaching RFP deadline fuels the fires of activity.

> **RFP (Request for Proposal)**
>
> Government's declaration that it's going to buy something. It contains specifications about what's wanted and what rules must be followed. They may be simple or highly complex but even the simple ones are almost always confusing.
>
> An **RFP** is commonly called a "bid" or a "tender". There are other variations, sometimes called a **Request for Quotation** or **RFQ** and **Request for Information** or **RFI**, depending on the agency involved.

In the less RFP-oriented company, emphasis is placed on understanding needs early on, establishing strong value propositions, proving themselves at every turn, and gracefully walking away when they cannot help or cannot win.

The more selective relationship-driven RFP responder is growing. The RFP-driven company is shrinking.

A "passive-aggressive" sales strategy is a mistake.

Many times, companies use a "passive-aggressive" sales strategy. They passively wait for an RFP to be issued within the company's line of business. Then, once identified, they aggressively invest the attention and actions of hordes of people to figure out how to spin the company's response so their proposal is favored.

Don't misunderstand us. Responding to RFPs is certainly a requirement for playing in the government space and doing it effectively is both an art and a science. You'll likely never be able to eliminate RFP responses completely (more on this later); however, if the bulk of your opportunity development strategy is built around uncovering and responding to RFPs, yours will be a difficult ride.

Get in front of an RFP, not behind it.

It is imperative to understand that, at the RFP stage, specifications are set in stone and you're already too late to the party. Many times, preferences for a certain vendor have been well established. Plus, at the RFP stage, all of your competitors have the same information at the same time, and limited discovery can occur once the RFP is issued. And any questions posed to prospects must be shared with everyone. Not the ideal situation. No, our real goal is to get in front of prospects BEFORE specifications are developed so we can have an impact on the requirements before they're locked in. And, no, we're not talking about bid-rigging or exercising undue influence…far from it.

The ultimate picture of success here would be creating a sole source situation where competition is effectively excluded because your company is the only real option given the prospect's needs— needs you helped define after understanding their problems and objectives.

How, as a sales team, do you get in the door before the RFP is issued? It's all about relationship-building. Read on. Here's what you need to know.

Build relationships, emphasize commitment, and demonstrate trust.

When we talk about relationships in government sales, we're not talking about making buddies and BFFs of the people involved in government buying, (although we enjoy the relationships we've built over the years with many of our government customers). We're talking more about relationships that genuinely serve the mutual needs of everyone involved. They don't have to be especially friendly relationships, but they do need to be ones where a foundation of trust has been forged and a structure of reliance and competence has been built.

"Isn't that true of selling to anyone?" you ask.

Yes, you're right to some degree…but it's more acute in government sales. People in a position to buy something, or more accurately, recommend something be bought by the government are not risk-takers. In the first place, they generally take very seriously their duty to spend tax money wisely. Those who don't do so won't stay in a position to buy long. They may not lose their jobs. They may not be demoted. They may not even know they've lost their clout, but lose it they will.

People who buy stuff for the government know their decisions will be closely watched by many people. In some cases, votes can be lost, or worse, people can literally suffer injury because of bad government buys. Government buyers (and when we say buyers, we don't mean just the people who have "buyer" in their title; we mean anyone involved in the process) know that, if they make a mistake, it will not be a quiet mistake. They know their mistakes stick even if they do well the next quarter. Government moves at a slower pace than the private sector. That means, when a mistake is made, it takes longer for people to forget about them.

So, it only makes sense that folks in the government want to do business with people and companies they trust. Trust only comes through a positive relationship. Sometimes these relationships take years to establish. Other times they can be established in a first meeting.

What we're about to discuss is information from some pretty heavy-duty research on how business relationships are formed. Much of the information here stems from work conducted by Robert Morgan and Shelby Hunt in the area of relationship marketing.[1]

While research details can get pretty hairy when delving into psychological processes such as this, we will simplify the findings to provide realistic and practical advice on building relationships and trust with prospects and other business partners – particularly in the government space.

The first question you may ask is, "What exactly do we mean by relationship commitment?"

The definition Morgan & Hunt offer is a pretty good one:

> ***Relationship Commitment***—*An exchange partner believing that an ongoing relationship with another is so important as to warrant maximum efforts at maintaining it; that is, the committed party believes the relationship is worth working on to ensure it endures indefinitely.*

That sounds about right to us. After all, from both a corporate and individual selling standpoint, our ultimate goal should be to create lasting relationships with our customers—relationships so valuable they will expend their own energy to sustain it.

A few years ago, a large, prestigious customer from a law enforcement agency visited us and the company we were representing. We paraded him in front of Mr. K, the CEO, knowing the customer would sing our praises and make us look good to the boss. Imagine our shock when the customer said, "Mr. K, your company has let me down."

---

[1] The Commitment-Trust Theory of Relationship Marketing"; Robert M. Morgan & Shelby D. Hunt; Journal of Marketing, July 1994; page 20.

We squirmed. We wondered what in the heck we did wrong. We had been working hard to make this persnickety customer happy. He continued by telling Mr. K, "I invest a lot of time and effort into building a relationship with a vendor, and I don't let many penetrate our walls. I'm very selective, and your company is one of the ones I hand-picked, but here's where you let me down...you've not come back to sell me anything else!" Mr. K started squirming at that point, knowing we had been pushing him for more product to sell.

Our customer and other people of influence in the government have a lot on their plates. Forget about the stories you hear of government people constantly goofing off on the job. Yes, government has some hacks, like private businesses do, but these are not the people to whom you are selling. Goof-offs don't find themselves in a position to buy, or to recommend buying. Their bosses and colleagues make sure they don't. Besides, it's as difficult, if not more so, to buy something in the government as it is to sell something to the government. Lazy government workers don't want the hassle.

The people you want to influence are movers-and-shakers. They're the ones with power, the ones like our visiting customer. And, they place a high value on trust and relationships.

Government customers with clout will actually *help* you sell to them. If they trust you and value the relationship, they will be your coaches. They will let you know what they want, and why. They'll guide you through the maze you're going to face. They won't let pesky lower-priced competitors come between the two of you (even when pricing must be particularly competitive). Customers like these will keep buying from you over and over. Since they take their responsibilities seriously, they would be reckless not doing so.

So, understanding the factors affecting customer commitment could be very beneficial, right? We absolutely think so, too.

We can't go much further into the discussion without defining trust:

> **Trust**—*the willingness to rely on an exchange partner in whom one has confidence.*

As you might expect, the amount of trust that exists between two parties has a major impact on the level of relationship commitment and involvement. Trust is central to commitment, but technically it is also a concept that stands on its own. Trust and commitment are two sides of the same coin to some degree. Increase your level of relationship commitment and trust, and you've got yourself a long-term customer you can't beat off with a stick.

Strong commitment & trust yield four benefits.

Before we dig into the key drivers of relationship commitment and trust, let's first take a look at what focusing on these two things will get you. Technically, these are often referred to as "outcomes." Research has shown there are some pretty nifty benefits to making concerted efforts at building relationship commitment and trust.

Benefit #1: Greater "Acquiescence." Acquiescence is not a pretty term as we hard-charging, independent types don't typically like the idea of "acquiescing' to anything. And, we have made it pretty clear our sales approach should not be coercive in nature. However, it's an accurate description of one of the relationship benefits. Take a look at how Morgan and Hunt define the term.

> **Acquiescence**—*the degree to which a relationship partner accepts or adheres to another's specific requests or policies.*

We hope prospects will take our advice and *acquiesce* to our requests related to buying our products. With channel partners or distributors, we expect them to actively promote our products and *conform* to certain policies and procedures. Stronger relationship commitment and trust will yield a greater likelihood of compliance with these desires.

It should be noted that such acquiescence doesn't stem from abusive power. Acquiescence through intimidation or coercion is a hallmark of dysfunction. However, in healthy relationships, we frequently find ourselves bowing to the other party's wishes ("Yes, dear."). We do so because we value the relationship and desire for it to continue. This is the "right" kind of acquiescence that stems from positive relationship bonds.

Benefit #2: Lower Propensity to Leave. No you haven't just turned on an episode of Dr. Phil. We are still talking about building relationships and the benefits of doing so within a government selling environment. In this case, "propensity to leave" is not about showing up at your house to find your clothes, your collection of vinyl records from the 70's and your flat-screen TV in a pile on the front yard while your significant other is escaping to Tijuana to "find themselves". It is about a customer, prospect or channel partner's decision not to buy or continue a partnership.

The research shows, as one would expect, buyers and business partners are less likely to seek another source for their desired product or service, and conversely more likely to hang around and spend money when there is a strong relationship commitment and trust. (As in our "Mr. K" example above.)

Benefit #3: Better Cooperation. The research shows greater relationship commitment enhances cooperation and coordination among two business-focused parties. Whether a new prospect or long-time channel partner, cooperation is needed to achieve virtually any desired result.

Cooperation is really a "higher order" outcome more than mere acquiescence. With acquiescence, only the most basic level of participation will occur—just enough interaction to get by. When a spirit of cooperation has been sown and cultivated, the fruit is a true collaborative partnership, with both of you pursuing the means to achieve a set goal.

For example, in the case of a channel partner, the company may begrudgingly yield to contractual requirements for advertising your product. When cooperating, they may actually proactively suggest new messages and media for advertising—fulfilling the role of a truly engaged business partner.

Benefit #4: More Productive Conflict. Productive conflict? Do we really want conflict from prospects, customers and channel partners? The answer is a resounding "YES!" In any relationship, there will be disagreements and differing viewpoints. The goal should not be to eliminate these divergent opinions, but instead harness and leverage them.

When there is strong relationship commitment and trust between parties, conflict can produce ideas and innovations that would have never arisen otherwise. The benefit of working through difficult times will have lasting positive effects. In fact, the time to start worrying the most is not when conflict arises, but when no one cares enough about the relationship to raise a fuss.

Besides, you'll find many government decision-makers are crusty types. They appreciate candor, even disagreements, more than "suck up sales types". There have been many times when disagreements and differing viewpoints, expressed properly, showed me a government buyer was buying into what we had to say.

[Rick] I was recently in a meeting with a senior official of a state police agency. He was a cantankerous guy by nature and skeptical by training. He took me to task more than once, then very openly questioned my motivations for doing something significantly less expensively than others, who would have charged a pretty penny. I quietly fumed and let him go on. After the meeting, I asked to speak to him privately in the hall. For a short guy without a gun and badge talking to a tall guy with a gun and badge, I explained to him in very clear terms why I was motivated to do the work for as little as I was charging. I laid out two very reasonable things I wanted from him in exchange. I also told him that I had been asked to do the work as a favor for a staffer of his I had known for years. His tone changed immediately. I got what I wanted. He got what he wanted. This senior official is now an ally, a very good and important one. We had just gone through productive conflict.

Then, there was the time I rather forcefully suggested to a big group of U.S. Postal Service buyers that we could use FedEx to ship the product I was trying to sell to the Postal Service to post offices across the country. Umm, not such a productive conflict.

Strategies for Building Commitment & Trust

Now that we've seen the benefits of focusing on relationship-building, let's dissect business relationships and discover the steps to building better commitment and trust. The discussion points here apply to all manner of government business relationships, ranging from prospects, to customers, to channel partners.

Strategies for Building Commitment & Trust

Strategy 1: Discover and Nurture Shared Values.

Shared values are simply beliefs or principles commonly agreed upon between exchange partners (customers, prospects, channel partners, etc.). Strong shared values indicate two people are like-minded with regards to what is important or unimportant, and what is right or wrong.

While "shared values" sound like deep, complex sets of beliefs, they can be fairly mundane interests like sports, hobbies or activities if they are truly important to the exchange partner. The common interest could be a certain volunteer creative problem-solving program for students. (Shameless plug for my pet volunteer organization, Destination ImagiNation®.) Interestingly, research has shown shared values is the *only* component to impact both relationship commitment *and* trust at the same time.

It is a concept with which we are all familiar. Each of us has met people with whom we've "hit it off" very quickly. Many times, the connection is made due to the discovery of some belief, practice or principle shared between us. This can be as superficial as recognizing the person sitting next to you on a plane uses the same brand of computer, or as deep as finding yourself in the middle of a crisis and discovering another person shares your same religious views.

Leverage shared values to enhance sales performance. If you've been in sales for any length of time, you have probably heard the rapport-building advice that upon entering a prospect's office, you should look for ways to connect with what is important to him/her on an individual level. Pictures of family on his desk? Talk about your kids. Golf trophies on her bookshelf? Tell her about your trip to Pebble Beach. These cues are indicators of some interest or value that could provide a connection point.

The goal, according to traditional thinking, is to establish personal rapport through aligning oneself with the prospect's interest. It's decent advice on the surface, as honing in on prospect passions is clearly an effective method for easing initial introductions.

However, deeper relationship building requires expanding this practice beyond the initial meeting. Salespeople should move past thinking the method is just an ice-breaking gimmick. Instead, *focus on ways to build a deeper shared value framework* between you as the seller and your prospect or partner over the long-term.

Even though there's little, if no, wining and dining in government sales, shared values can still be established in short order. Those who influence government buying are generally passionate, multi-faceted, and interesting people. They don't mind talking about their interests, and will appreciate your interest…as long as it's not forced or insincere.

Practically, what steps do we take to make this work? Here are some key steps in the process:

Leveraging Shared Values

- **Observe**. Make a concerted and discreet effort to become more aware of interests and values.
- **Capture**. Make notes about the interests/values you uncover and capture these in your contact database for future reference.
- **Review**. Revisit the values you have observed and captured for your entire prospect list regularly so you'll keep them fresh in your mind.
- **Collect**. Be on constant lookout for things you know will pique your prospects' interest or tap into mutually shared values. Simple things like news articles or pertinent websites are great.
- **Share**. Commit to passing along content that will be of interest to prospects and reinforce shared values. Don't make a big deal out of your efforts, and don't try to squeeze in a heavy sales pitch. Just an "I saw this and thought of you" will suffice. Even if you didn't write it, pass it along.

Heck, we've even passed along helpful information from a competitor. We were remembered quite fondly for providing the information.

- **Be Genuine.** Trying to "force" shared values where none really exist will backfire on you. It is certainly fine to appear interested in your prospect's passion for Bavarian enamel dinner plates, but pretending to have that same love without any real emotional tie will be easily detected, ultimately working against you. Even if you don't have a mutual level of interest in something, recognition of its importance to the prospect will go a long way.

You'll be amazed at how much mileage you'll get from tuning into shared values. Practicing the simple steps outlined here will impress prospects and customers with your attention to detail and your personal interest.

Strategy 2: Build Relationship Benefits.

A second way to enhance relationship commitment is to *focus on creating clearly recognizable relationship benefits.* Simply put, relationship benefits relate to the old "what's in it for me" question in a business relationship. While prospects and partners don't want to feel you are only hanging around for your own selfish personal gain (we'll discuss this more later), they don't have any trouble desiring something from the relationship for themselves.

Relationship benefits stem from a variety of areas. Let's place ourselves in the shoes of the prospect or partner and examine just a few of the more powerful ones:

Knowledge/Expertise. As a prospect, I might derive benefit from a relationship with you if you bring unique knowledge or expertise to the table that will make my life easier or make me look good to people important to me. This is a very important one. Sooner or later, with every purchase or every project, a government buyer is going to need to demonstrate to bosses that she knows enough about the topic to make the right decision, and avoid missteps. One of the smartest things you can do to build your relationship with a government buyer is to look for ways you can provide knowledge and expertise to make your prospect look smarter. This cannot be over-emphasized. IT WORKS!

Future Gain. I might want to build a relationship with you if I can foresee some future role you might play in my life. Perhaps someday you'll reveal your secret fishing spot to me (no, forget it, our lips are sealed) or I will hit you up for a job reference. Government workers often have a life-after-government in the private sector. As they become more senior, and generally more influential, they are thinking about their life in the wonderful world of private enterprise where riches seem to exist. While this can be a taboo topic, it does exemplify future gain. (Being reckless about this topic risks making your prospect very uncomfortable. You might even violate laws and rules.)

Mutual Connection. I might find it beneficial to develop a relationship with you if we share a mutual relationship (particularly one of some importance to me). If you're best friends with my boss' wife, it would behoove me to play nice.

Network Access. This is similar to the mutual connection benefit source, except you and I may not *currently* share a connection. I might find it beneficial to have a relationship with you because I know you're well-connected to others whose interests parallel mine.

Fame or notoriety. Sometimes it's just cool to carefully say you know someone due to their status or notoriety. I might desire a relationship with you because you are a known success in your industry, you write a widely-read blog, you just won an Oscar, or wrote a cool book about selling to government.

Examine closely each of the possible benefits above for clues on how to enhance prospect or partner relationship benefits. These sources of relationship benefits rarely occur by themselves, but are instead typically interconnected. In fact, the best strategy to employ as a salesperson is to create and leverage as many of these benefits as possible in tandem.

Take, for example, your humble authors and our approach to building relationship benefits for our sales and marketing consulting business—Galain Solutions, Inc. (Hey, it's our book. We get to plug it.)

We have extensive experience and success leading government sales and marketing organizations which validates and reinforces our potential to offer solid **knowledge/expertise**. We have published this book, are regular contributors to a variety of professional trade magazines, and have received media attention because of our expertise. This enhances our **fame/notoriety**. Because of our experience, reputation and other efforts, we have developed a strong **network** of government sales professionals and government officials. With a strong network comes a high likelihood that we share a **mutual connection** with our prospects. This is, indeed, a regular occurrence for us particularly in certain segments of the market in which we have deep experience. Finally, considering all these elements together, it is reasonable for a prospect to conclude there might be some **future gain** to be realized by working closely with us through a consulting engagement (they would be right).

Let's bring this concept a little closer to home for you personally. If you remember our discussion on pairing personal brand traits with content, you'll recall we urged you to push to prospects helpful content that supports their values/interests and reinforces your own key messages. Not only does this effort help position you as a trusted source, and reduce your reliance on cold-calling, it also becomes a way to *enhance relationship benefits*.

This method is so powerful it even works when personal selling is not involved—namely online sales. Think about the process you might go through in choosing and acquiring an online sales training program, for instance.

It starts with conducting key word searches. From the small description provided on the search page, you click on a program that interests you. On the company's website, you will typically find background on the creator of the program or the company itself. You're impressed with the credentials, though you are not quite ready to make a commitment. However, your interest is piqued enough to provide the company with an email address in exchange for a monthly sales-focused newsletter.

Over time, the sales seminar company may feed you bits of helpful information and useful sales tips. Eventually, you come to trust the seminar provider's point of view, and you may order the selling program. As you experience and apply the information, you become a dedicated disciple. You may even seek to network with others who subscribe to the same methods and philosophies through social networking sites or other means.

When the seminar company offers a new sales education product, you've benefitted so much by your previous experience, you are ready to buy whatever they're selling.

Do you see what has happened and how relationship benefits have developed over time? Can you see how content plays a critical role in this? In this example, relationship commitment has developed between you and the sales training provider, even though you may have never even spoken to another human being in the process.

Strategy 3: Make it Expensive to Terminate the Relationship.

A third way to build deeper exchange partner relationship commitment is to increase relationship termination costs—that is, ratcheting up the "price" one might pay for ending the alliance. While this strategy must be deployed with sensitivity and caution, it can be an effective method for solidifying relationship bonds.

In any business relationship, there is a cost connected with ending the association. Sometimes, the cost is near zero, while other times the cost can be quite high.

For example, on the low side, consider the termination costs of switching toothpaste. While some people may defend to the death their choice of brands, for most of us, there is relatively little pain or inconvenience in switching to another offering. From a toothpaste manufacturer's perspective, termination costs are very low. There is relatively little pain Procter & Gamble can inflict on you should you decide to ditch your tube of Crest® for the siren call of a competing brand.

On the high termination cost side, consider Southwest Airlines (the "company plane" for many of us road warriors) and its association with Boeing. Southwest's entire fleet of aircraft is comprised of some variant of the Boeing 737. Fleet standardization is a fundamental part of Southwest's overall business strategy as having a single-model fleet allows them to keep costs low through uniform training, maintenance, operating procedures, etc. Imagine the "termination costs" of switching airplane suppliers in Southwest Airline's case. At this point, it would be nigh impossible.

Clearly, relationship termination costs can have a strong impact on relationship commitment. In business, termination costs are frequently contractual, but emotional and psychological termination costs are also very real and very powerful.

Termination Costs as a Strategy

Companies and salespeople should look for ways to increase the "pain" associated with a prospect buying from another vendor, or with a customer switching solutions. We are NOT saying salespeople should invent ways to maliciously punish prospects for not buying or customers for leaving. We're saying DON'T do that. On rare occasions, we have seen an angry salesperson attempt to seek petty retribution for losing a fair deal. This is ridiculous, unprofessional behavior that should never be tolerated in any circumstance. (It also does not work.)

Instead, salespeople should make sure:

1) The rules of engagement and *disengagement* are clearly defined for all parties involved, and

2) Such clear value and problem resolution is delivered to the exchange partner that it would be uncomfortable for them to no longer have access to it.

One way to achieve this is through *contractual agreements*—a formalized approach to termination cost management (part of the salesperson's "rules of disengagement" responsibility). Take your cell phone provider as an example. If you read the fine print of the contract you've signed, you will see it allows you to terminate your service before the contract term expires. However, you will also see there's a hefty fee to pay if you do it. Unless you're really miffed at the provider, you'll probably just keep the service until the contract expires because the termination costs are too high.

On the flip side, formal contractual *incentives* may also be used to increase termination costs. For instance, some companies offer discounts for first-time buyers, or enhanced customer support options that may only be available in exchange for a renewed or extended purchase agreement. Even government buyers dislike passing on "deals" when they can get them. As such, there is a cost associated with passing up these special offers, even if it manifests itself in the form of an incentive.

Contracts aside, termination cost as a strategy may not be as tough as you would expect. There are inherent reasons why this is not true. Go back to "Mr. K". Remember how our customer complained that we didn't offer him anything else to buy after his hard work agreeing to buy from us in the first place. Government buyers generally don't enter into their relationships lightly. They are cautious. There is too much at stake for them to act otherwise. Missteps can result in serious consequences, even loss of, heaven forbid, votes. With so much invested, government buyers do not terminate their relationships lightly.

So, there are steps that can be taken to increase termination costs. Think about the list of possible relationship benefits we all seek: knowledge/expertise, future gain, mutual connection, network access, fame/notoriety. If you have been really successful in building any of these elements with a prospect or partner, then the removal of these could carry with it a certain degree of pain— clearly a termination cost. It is actually possible for a salesperson to serve as such a valuable source of positive benefits that the exchange partner would be negatively impacted by the loss of the personal connection.

A word of caution is in order here. You should be very careful with the deployment of this particular strategy. If a line is crossed and the customer perceives "coercion" is taking place, you'll weaken the relationship, not strengthen it. The exchange partner may put up with you as long as absolutely necessary, then drop you like a hot potato at the first opportunity. No one likes to feel manipulated or forced into a corner. Deployed gingerly, however, increasing termination costs can be a useful component of an overall relationship-building plan.

Strategy 4: Improve Communication Quality & Quantity

A fourth strategy for building deeper business relationships is to *enhance efforts surrounding communications.* Communication is a major driver of trust and critical to developing overall relationship commitment. This is particularly true working with government. Theirs is a very documentation/communication-driven world. Nothing gets done without a lot of documentation, thus communication. A smart government sales or business development person uses this sometimes frustrating reality to her advantage. She communicates lots of relevant information that helps her prospects provide the mound of documentation usually required to get just about anything in government done.

We are certainly not blazing any new trails with this particular topic. Libraries and bookstores are filled with books on the "how's and why's" of better communication. We wish we had a nickel for every time the issue of improving communications was brought up at company meetings and planning sessions over the years.

It's crazy, isn't it? Never before in the history of the world have humans been so connected to one another through so many different communications options. Landline phones, Blackberries®, Bluetooth® devices, multiple email accounts, SMS, Instant Messaging, VoIP calling, Twitter accounts, LinkedIn, Facebook,...and that just lists the communication methods of my thirteen year-old daughter.

Still, communication continues to be one of the most significant obstacles to successful relationship-building in a business environment. Why, in today's world of hyper-communications, is this still such a problem? Perhaps we'll write another book on this topic. In the meantime, here is how contemporary communications can become an obstacle to relationship building.

We can become overwhelmed by an information deluge.

It's no secret we're all absolutely flooded with information. The sheer volume of data directed at us on a daily basis makes it difficult to sort through the meaningful nuggets of real communication.

We are connected to more people through more devices, but have less time.

OK, we all still have 24 hours in a day so "less time" isn't technically accurate. However it certainly feels that way. While advertisers and other people we *don't* even know are drowning us with attempts to communicate, everyone we *do* know has multiple devices and communications channels available to use to drown us as well. We are expected to be reachable at any moment in time and there is a marked increase in the amount of duplication of effort associated with using all these many devices. Have you ever wasted time deleting mobile phone voice mail, home phone voice mail, SMS and email all from the same person who has tried multiple ways to reach you? This leads us to the next problem.

We are forced into increased reactive communications.

Before your authors were entrepreneurs and sales gurus, we were standard corporate types. We know personally there were times it seemed as if our whole day was spent simply responding to unplanned urgent email or voicemail requests. It was as if our entire work schedule was dictated by what popped up in Microsoft Outlook®, as opposed to us "planning the work, and working the plan." We have a feeling many of you can relate. With greater accessibility and an exponential increase in communications options and devices, we frequently communicate in reactive mode—that is in response to someone else's urgency. It's not always a bad thing, but it can lead to communication shortcuts and heightened frustrations that inhibit meaningful interactions and collaborative exchanges.

We must deal with an explosive increase in the quantity of useless information.

With all the craziness just described, one would think each of us would be cautious and conservative with the volume of information we produce and consume. However, just the opposite is happening. We've become addicted to information as a society, having an insatiable desire for more.

Take Twitter, for example. We're certainly not opposed to Twitter: we use the service ourselves and believe it offers some redeeming qualities and positive benefits. However, one can only imagine the billions of bits of completely useless information traveling the IP superhighway on an hourly basis. At some point, the wasted time associated with the creation and consumption of all this dribble is going to have a negative effect on society and our national (if not global) productivity. At a minimum, it is another distraction and something else to which we must respond (increasing reactive communications). Clearly, *more* communication is not necessarily *better* communication.

We must communicate exactly what we mean without actually saying anything.

A final thought on why communication is difficult today relates to our movement toward non-verbal communication. Not to say we're more animated in our gestures when talking. I mean we're relying more on textual methods such as email (for us old folks over the age of 35) and texting to disseminate our messages. In some cases, the written word is preferred over verbal interactions. It is frequently better to think through a communication or response and carefully "put it in writing" as opposed to popping off at the mouth.

However, given the communication environment just described, we often *don't* think through responses carefully because there simply isn't time (ten more messages just arrived in our inbox). Or, we're limited to 160 characters in a text message to get our point across. This often leads to misunderstandings and miscommunications as contextual clues such as voice inflection, facial expressions are not a part of the communication stream.

It is a mistake to think these misunderstandings only happen with close friends and co-workers. Interchanges with prospects and partners are just as susceptible to problems caused by text-oriented communications.

Three Ways to Improve Communication

So, given the challenges of communicating in today's world, how do we create outstanding interpersonal connections with prospects in order to enhance our relationship? There are many factors. However, we believe there are three main components that must exist before solid communications with exchange partners can occur: relevance, timeliness and reliability.

Be Relevant. Simply providing information to prospects is not, within itself, enough to enhance communications and further the relationship. The information exchanged must be perceived as being relevant to the respective recipients. This is even more important in today's world where information overload is reaching SPAMdemic proportions.

As salespeople, we must be selective with regards to the information we attempt to push to prospects. Approaching each and every outreach, we should ask ourselves, "Will this information truly and uniquely answer a prospect question or help solve a prospect problem?" If not, you're likely wasting your time and making little headway cultivating a deeper relationship. If so, you're on your way to making a new BFF.

Be Timely. The timing of the information exchange is also critical to its impact on relationship development. Really good outreach efforts at a really bad time in the life of a prospect will at best, be ignored, and at worst, create a perception that you are self-serving and insensitive. Many times, it's impossible to know whether or not your communication efforts are coming at a good time or not. So ask. Simple courtesies such as asking, "Is this a good time to talk about this?" or, "Would this information be helpful to you?" will be appreciated.

Be Reliable. This piece of the communications pie can only be illustrated over time. Great communication doesn't happen overnight, but instead improves as interactions occur over time as information exchanges are proven accurate and dependable. While we may not be able to remember details of each of these interactions, our minds appear to be able to store assessments of these various touch points. Thus, we develop overall feelings about certain people and whether or not their word can be trusted.

While it's impossible to do justice to the topic of communications in the context of this particular book, the simple practice of *focusing* on relevant, timely and reliable communications methods will help overcome barriers to personal interaction and improve overall relationship commitment and trust.

Considering their need for information and documentation to avoid trouble down the road, government buyers are particularly appreciative of reliable information.

Strategy 5: Minimize perceived selfish behavior.

A final factor influencing relationship commitment is the prospect's *interpretation* of a salesperson's opportunistic behavior—that is--how much of our relationship is "*you* wanting something from *me*."

We all understand relationships, even very intimate ones, have some "selfish" dimension to them. The buyer-seller relationship is certainly no exception. That's alright to a degree--prospects aren't really looking for a new best friend--they realize you're getting paid to be nice to them.

However, even in the buyer-seller scenario where a certain degree of tolerance towards self-centered thinking exists, a line can be crossed where the prospect believes a salesperson's only REAL interest is himself. If a buyer believes the salesperson is willing to do or say anything in order to close a deal, you've got a recipe for relationship disaster.

Each of us, at some time or another, has likely encountered an obnoxious salesperson that succeeded in pushing a product or service on us that didn't really meet our needs. We've probably all experienced the feeling of being duped by some idiot who made unrealistic promises to meet his sales quota for the day.

Few things anger us more than an experience like this. It leaves us feeling betrayed, stupid and even guilty for not seeing through the charade. Psychologically, these are some pretty strong negative emotions we'd prefer to avoid. So, like pulling our hand away from a hot stove, once burned, prospects and partners withdraw themselves from a relationship at the first hint that a salesperson is being contriving and manipulative.

People who work in government are particularly sensitive to the "in it for me" sales or business development person. We believe most government employees, particularly those in a position to make buying decisions, consider themselves on a mission. They believe they are doing more than making a living. They are doing their duty by serving in the government when they could be in the private sector making more money, working shorter hours, and dealing with fewer politicians. (Generally speaking, they're right.) So, if they're doing their duty, they expect people they buy from to do theirs. (Right again.)

Build a relationship without being obvious.

Our goal in developing deeper relationship commitment is to minimize any chance the prospect will feel our motives are strictly selfish. How do we do this?

Simply look for ways to help a prospect or partner achieve their goals with no expectation for an immediate payback.

For a prospect, it might be volunteering to help with a charity in which they are involved (and one for which you have a true calling to help) or buying a box of Girl Scout cookies they're selling for their daughter. For a dealer or channel partner, it might be helping search for a needed employee or offering to help staff a trade show booth. There are endless ways one can help others that do not cost much (or do not run contrary to procurement rules) if you keep your eyes open.

The die-hard skeptics among you might suggest these offers to "help" are just thinly disguised gimmicks to try and ingratiate oneself to a prospect. These curmudgeons might say prospects will see through these insincere attempts and perceive this to be yet another method for manipulation—ultimately turning off the prospect.

Our best response to this is, "You might be right." To us, it all depends on your state of mind and heart when seeking to help. We're not saying all selfish intentions can or should be completely erased from the equation. But we also believe most people can sense when motives are reasonably pure and when they are tainted with false sincerity. We think there are times when salespeople and others should simply "do something good" to make a situation or person better. Certain jaded prospects may view your actions with skepticism. That's OK. Others will conclude your efforts are genuine and you're actually a decent human being. They may not buy from you immediately, but you've planted a relationship seed and you've made the world a little better through your actions.

A word of caution is in order here. Please use good judgment when attempting to deploy this "strategy." Even when your motives are pure, the actions you take could be misinterpreted by others, (perhaps outside of the prospect) getting you into trouble professionally and legally. For example, writing a fat check to a prospect's favorite charity might be perceived as a "you scratch my back, I'll scratch yours" arrangement. When in doubt, ask the prospect and your management where lines of propriety should be drawn.

A desire to help others achieve their goals without the promise of immediate personal payback will, no doubt, help build relationship commitment and trust. Ultimately, good sales karma will follow you down the road when a little selflessness is a part of the game plan.

A Final Thought on Relationship Building

There are no shortcuts to using the relationship building strategies discussed in this chapter. They are not easy and results do not happen overnight. (Hey, you're the one who decided to get into government sales.)

However, the long sales cycles typical in most government selling situations actually work to our advantage here. Unlike some sales professionals, government salespeople do not have to build rapport, establish trust and close a sale within a sixty-minute window. You may have months—even years—to create deeper connections with your buyers and partners. Don't waste it.

You can scurry about frantically responding to RFPs you had no influence in or over, or you can work a real relationship development plan using the insights we've discussed, benefiting from a deeper personal connections and true consultative perspective. We choose relationships over RFPs to drive success in government business every time.

SAGE ADVICE

Saying "Thanks"

In the corporate world, it's not unusual to send a customer a small token of appreciation for their business, particularly around certain holidays. But, in the government world, you risk running afoul of strict government policies on receiving gifts. So how do you say "thank you" without breaking any procurement rules? Here are a few suggestions not limited to a single season of the year:

Send a handwritten note. Handwritten notes are clearly an underutilized and meaningful way to express gratitude to customers. In today's world of email and text-messaging, an actual signature is a rare and beautiful thing.

Send nuggets of helpful information throughout the year. This is not a difficult task and doesn't cost a thing. The form of a newsletter is OK, but even better is a personal email with links to specific and helpful information. It lets customers know you are thinking about them and their unique needs. Don't be discouraged if they do not respond with their thanks to you for providing information.

Give customers exclusive access to important product or company information prior to its public release (if possible). *[Lorin]* This year, as a way of saying thanks for being a Best Buy "Silver Member" customer, I received an email giving me access to Black Friday electronics specials *before* they were released to the general public. Good stuff. I felt appreciated and took advantage of the opportunity.

While this specific example is not completely applicable to government procurement situations, the principle remains the same. Look for ways of sharing internal information (product releases, training opportunities, etc.) to customers in a special or exclusive way as a means for making them feel appreciated (NOTE: Please make sure this is an approved corporate program-- not a sharing of any insider corporate secrets.)

Remember, government buyers don't take their vendor relationships lightly. They are scrutinized in many ways for the vendor relationships they establish. Once they've established them, they don't mind efforts to maintain them.

Also, don't be surprised if your efforts are not acknowledged immediately. This doesn't mean they're not noticing. Many times, we thought we were being unheard only to get a call at the end of the fiscal year saying, "Hey, we've got some money left over to spend. Do you think you could freshen up that proposal and get it over to me, say, in fifteen minutes?" (They were listening after all.)

Follow up. Many times, we as salespeople are guilty of "hit and runs." We make a sale, and then run to the next prospect, leaving customers feeling abandoned and under-appreciated. Even if you must hand-off the account to a customer relations department, take the time to follow up on how the project implementation is going or call to see how satisfied the customer is with your product or service. Such interest shows sincere appreciation and concern for maintaining a long-term relationship.

Listen. Most importantly, keep your eyes and ears open. Pay attention to what's going on with your customers and prospects. Understand. If you don't, ask questions.

Seven Myths Take-Aways

- By building relationships, you can get in front of an RFP, not come in behind it.

- Your relationship with a purchaser will demonstrate those qualities and benefits that make your company attractive to a buyer.

- Effective and valuable communication must be relevant, timely, useful, and consistent.

- The sales cycle in government business is a long one, you'll sell more and more often when you get in early and stay through the end.

- Strategies for building commitment & trust:
    - Discover and nurture shared values.
    - Build and remind prospects of relationship benefits.
    - Increase termination costs.
    - Improve the quality and quantity of communications.
    - Eliminate perceptions that you're just "in it for yourself."

CHAPTER TWO

MYTH #2: Cold calling is king.

FACT #2: Content is king.

[Lorin] My first job out of college was selling new and used cars for a Ford dealership in Nashville, TN. It was on a frigid January Monday morning during a recession when I, along with nine other fresh-faced sales "pledges," donned our one sports coat and tie and started work.

The first three days were spent immersed in Ford Motor Company's official training class for sales representatives. We were quickly exposed to sales principles and practices such as: qualifying prospects during the trade-in test drive, "mirroring" physical behaviors to establish rapport, the infamous "If I can get you the deal you want on this car, will you buy today?" trial-close. We were also briefed on the company's sales culture and pecking order–making sure we paid proper homage to our deities-in-residence: the owner, the finance manager and the sales manager.

With completion certificates in hand, avoiding the sneers and hazing of the old-timers, we hit the showroom floor, eager to apply our newfound knowledge to the next vehicularly-challenged prospect. Only we didn't stay on the showroom floor for long.

The recession was taking its toll on dealership foot traffic. Unproductive, inexperienced, draw-earning, chain-smoking sales people were devouring profits through time wasting and mass coffee consumption ("coffee is for *closers*" after all). So, after two hours, we were ushered into our fish-tank-like "offices" by the crusty sales manager and given what was supposed to be the Holy Grail of sales resources – the almighty telephone White Pages. Our goal was simple--call through our assigned alphabetical section of the book and try to convince some poor schmuck to leave the comfort of his warm couch and trudge through the icy slop for some quality face-time with an overzealous car salesman. It was the first time I recall hearing the phrase "smiling and dialing," though I can assure you little actual smiling occurred on either end of the telephone.

For the next several days, we repeated the pattern of dialing, regurgitating a script, experiencing rejection, hanging up, and dialing again:

"Mr. Laban, this is Lorin Bristow with Acme Ford Dealership. May I ask what kind of car you now drive? – Funny, I know a person just dying to buy a 1972 Pinto…want to trade it in?"

"Ms. Lendale, this is Lorin Bristow with Acme Ford Dealership…Can't you just see yourself taking a vacation to the beach in a new car?...I had an appointment slot just open up for tomorrow…"

"Mr. Lowry, this is Lorin Bristow with Acme Ford… [click]…*Hello?...Hello?"*

Despite my youthful naiveté, I sensed this was not the path to fame and fortune. So, I began a small covert operation. When the service manager was away for lunch, I started pulling the carbon-copy records of customers who had recently serviced their vehicle. I looked specifically for customers servicing popular Ford models older than 3 years with no major service problems. I created a mail merge list of these individuals, saved them to a floppy disk the size of a pot-holder, and utilized the used car manager's DOS computer to print targeted, customized prospect letters.

I also began a networking campaign. I connected with friends and acquaintances, learning about their lives, telling them what I was doing, and asking for leads and referrals. When they referred a friend or relative, I thanked them heartily with a personal note.

Salesperson of the Year?

It would be a great ending to this story if I could say I was selected "Salesperson of the Year" as a result of these few simple actions. I was not. Seasoned old-timers pulling from a stable of past customers (some going back decades) sold many more vehicles than I. What I can say is, out of ten people in my initial sales class, only three of us survived for more than a few months. My efforts, simple as they were, produced results that far outpaced those who persisted in blind cold calling.

Though the car business ultimately proved not to be my cup of tea, it nevertheless taught me some very useful sales principles. Near the top of this list of lessons learned are the limitations of cold calling and the importance of CONTENT.

The Cold-Calling Conflict

As sales managers ourselves, we understand the conflict surrounding cold-calling. There are, after all, some actual benefits to cold calling in certain situations.

For example, with new or less-experienced salespeople, it offers the opportunity to overcome fear or anxiety while developing and polishing a concise "pitch." It's a good way to weed out ill-suited candidates. It gives neophytes who know squat about a product something to do other than take smoke breaks, manage fantasy football, and Twitter a play-by-play of their gastrointestinal movements. It certainly allows new salespeople the experience of persevering through rejection. And, as a rite of passage, it builds character while bonding team members together through adversity.

It is not, however, the most efficient and effective way for mature salespeople to drive government business over the long haul.

So if cold calling is out, what is in?

Lessons from a Rock Star

Ever wanted to be a rock star? As a musician for most of my life, I'll admit it has certainly crossed my mind. I recall my high-school talent show like it was yesterday. Mullet haircut. Sleeveless muscle shirt (minus the muscles). Parachute pants. Cheesy guitar crackling through a yard-sale Fender amplifier. Strutting and screeching the lyrics to ZZ-Top's "Sharp Dressed Man"—completely inaudible above the booming drum kit. The crowd seemed to love it, and so did I. We left the stage dreaming of limousines, money, MTV (they actually played music videos then) and seas of adoring fans of the feminine persuasion.

Later in life, I worked in marketing at the largest music licensing organization in the world. It was there I learned about the actual making of a rock star. I came to realize the glamour, hype, media attention and buzz were not showered on artists simply as a *reward* for achieving celebrity-status, but instead were elements of a deliberate approach aimed at convincing the public the artist was, in fact, *deserving* of star treatment.

It was not solely the *effect* of stardom; it was instead part of the *cause*. Record labels are masters at building momentum. Pairing a new act with a hot seller gives the fresh artist instant credibility while positioning them in the appropriate genre. This may entice music lovers to sample the artist's song on Apple iTunes®, follow them on Twitter, talk about them with friends, request their song on the radio, and ultimately buy the artist's music. (By the way, ask Rick about his son Patrick—a real rock star.)

This principle applies to you and your prospecting efforts as well. You are responsible not just for selling your company's product or service.

You are also responsible for selling YOU!! Your experience! Your expertise! Your time!

When you realize you are CEO of your own brand, you begin thinking differently. You start creating ways for prospects to be attracted to you rather than chasing them around like a love-sick teenager. You become a sales rock star riding a wave of momentum.

Creating Rock Star Momentum

Though it's not likely you'll be a global sensation overnight, creating substantial personal momentum is achievable. The steps involved in the process are as follows:
1. Define your unique Personal Brand Traits.
2. Pair your personal brand traits with content.
3. Cultivate a network of influencers and communicators.
4. Commit time to spreading the word.

Defining Personal Brand Traits

The first step in building your own brand is to figure out *what* about you *is* valuable. We're not talking about what makes you *employable*. We mean what is **valuable** and **unique** about you in relation to the products and services you are selling.

Are you a technical genius? Do you have presentation skills that make people swoon? Do you have many years of experience in your industry? Do you write well? Any of these things (let's call them "Personal Brand Traits") can be used as a foundation for building your personal sales brand.

Personal brand traits are unique abilities, personality characteristics or qualifications that make you stand out. In the same way a well-defined "unique selling proposition" helps sell products more effectively, so do clearly articulated qualities build a personal brand and enhance selling oneself (remember our goal here is to get out of the cold-calling rat race).

A few personal brand trait properties include:

- Specific technical expertise
- Achievement certifications
- Educational attainment/Degrees
- Past experience
- Speaking or writing ability
- Industry focus

Look for combinations of two or three traits that can be combined to **form a truly unusual and valuable set of properties**. Also, consider traits that are valuable to your *prospects*, not just to your current or future employer. Labeling oneself as the Genghis Kahn of sales negotiations might land you another selling job, but probably will not help you build an attractive reputation with prospects or decrease your reliance on cold-calling.

Examples:

Bill Smith:
- Former fire chief
- Industry association president
- Public safety product sales expertise
- Strong writing skills

Jane Jones:
- Professional public health-focused sales executive
- Chair of an industry health standards committee
- Volunteer at a physical rehab center for the elderly
- Strong public speaking skills

Jerry Downs:
- Former procurement officer for the Navy
- Software application developer
- Distribution channel specialist
- Social media expert

Pair Brand Traits with Content

Once you've identified the compelling properties of your personal brand, it is time to figure out how to leverage them as they relate to supplying the market with needed content. Content simply means information that is valued and consumed by your target audience.

For example, if you write well, find ways to use this to build personal notoriety and credibility. You might consider creating your own blog, developing a white paper, or offering your subject-matter expertise to trade magazines. This is particularly helpful in government sales. After all, somewhere along the process, someone to whom you want to sell is going to have to write a report, a justification, a sole source document, and/or a bid request. **Best that those words of wisdom are plagiarized from you!**

If public speaking is your thing, offer to present at conferences and webinars (record and video these when possible). Making presentations that are generous and truly valuable to your industry are not just sales pitches for your product. (Government buyers go to many conferences.) Remember, the goal is to build momentum so prospects see you as an expert resource instead of a selfish manipulator. Your brand builds a reputation as a giver not a taker.

When You're Not Ernest Hemingway

So how do you go about creating content if you're not quite Ernest Hemingway? The first place you might explore is your in-house marketing department. Despite the fact they live on a separate planet from you (more on this later), they generally have a sincere interest in helping you and the company be successful. Approach them in a respectful, collaborative manner. Offer to help create the message outline for whatever content you are creating. Propose to help connect them with other industry experts (customers for example) who might contribute quotes or other meaningful input. Then let them do their magic, turning your concept into a well-written, properly formatted document (or whatever you're creating).

Marketing will most likely be interested in investing in tools all salespeople in your organization can use, so don't expect too much special treatment. However, there is nothing wrong with other salespeople becoming rock stars in their territories as well, so encourage cross-department use and team up to add other skills to the mix. It won't hurt if your *content* is wide as well as deep. Collaboration with others whose expertise and association lends credibility and value to a prospect only enhances your *brand*.

Cultivate a Network of Influencers & Communicators

While you are building your repertoire of content, you will want to spend time cultivating a network of people who can help spread your message. It used to be, if one wanted to "network" with others for business purposes, he or she would attend a trade show, a hosted reception or some sort of sponsored educational event. Loaded down with business cards and drink tickets, a glad-handed, back-slapping salesperson would work the room, trolling for possible leads and prospects.

These events still occur, and they absolutely still have their place, but over the past decade ***online networking*** has exploded as a newer, more efficient means for connecting people. While slow in adopting some things, influential government workers generally network well.

Network Online

Over the last couple of years, more has been written about online networks than you can shake a stick at. Authors scream about Twitter, Facebook, LinkedIn, the necessity of blogging and other related topics. Many salespeople know they need to dig into this, but the payoff is not immediately evident, and they're too busy making those ever-so-productive cold calls. So they procrastinate.

While the topic is too deep to cover in detail within these pages, we would be remiss if we didn't throw our hat in the ring supporting these emerging tools...at least to a point.

Certainly trying to maintain and leverage every online networking tool cropping up these days is unrealistic. Simply adding your name and profile to these sites may not bear much sales fruit. However, wrapping the efforts we have discussed around content with a strong online content and networking strategy can pay big dividends.

For example, one specific practice area for Galain Solutions, Inc. relates to helping companies grow their business in the public safety technology space. Because of our expertise and the relationship network we have intentionally built (over time) we were chosen as featured bloggers for an award-winning public safety trade magazine.

Every week, we commit to creating relevant and insightful content surrounding this particular topic. While we receive no compensation for contributing to the publication, we are exposing our capabilities to thousands of readers every month. You can bet this has caused our phone to ring.

Commit Time to Spread the Word

Implementing this approach requires a commitment of time and resources. It is critical you carve out time each week to devote to these networking and content creating activities.

You may not be able to quit your cold calling cold turkey. However, if you can focus on personal branding/content strategy, two things will begin to happen. First, prospects will actually pick up the phone and call you (is this reverse-cold calling?). You may not be immediately deluged by adoring prospects waving signed contracts in your face, but over time prospect-initiated calls will happen with surprising regularity. **This is a beautiful thing**.

Second, when you do reach out to an unknown prospect, you have something to talk about other than how eagerly you want to relieve them of their budget dollars. You now have something of value to offer in exchange for small, but important bits of information.

For instance, the white paper can be offered in a voicemail in exchange for their email address and "opt-in" permission (so you can email them regularly without being accused of "spamming"). Trust us, properly presented, you will receive requests.

Government decision-makers read a lot as they work on their projects. If not really reading, they are looking for material to stuff in their files and email to their bosses to make it at least appear they've read a lot. Better that *your* white papers are in their folders and in-boxes than those of your *competitors*.

Access to an insightful play-on-demand webinar may be offered in exchange for agreeing to a brief personal telephone conversation. While the "you scratch my back, I'll scratch yours" aspects should be subtle, this exchange is fundamental to successful prospecting without cold calling.

While you're investing time and resources into getting attention for your content, don't forget to make sure your content is actually worthwhile. Give them something (make that lots of "somethings") they can really use, something that reflects the fact you understand their pain and have a suggestion for relief. Make the content so strong they will want to pass it along to their bosses. Think about how selective you are about forwarding documents to *your* boss.

Having people clamoring for your words of wisdom fares better than wasting your precious hours leaving voicemails that are never returned. Warning: what we're proposing here is actual work. Like most things related to government selling there is no quick-fix gimmick to magically open doors and place you in front of the right people.

You probably have balked at some of these ideas, maybe even said, "That's the marketing department's job." Go ahead. Hide behind the excuses. It's your income and your future.

We believe you are better than that. We believe you're not afraid to roll up your sleeves and get dirty. It's what attracted you to government sales in the first place.

But, don't try to eat the entire elephant at once.

Start today by defining your Personal Brand Traits. Then take steps daily to create content, develop your network and get the word out. **You can do this!**

Is that the crowd chanting your name I hear? Get out there and embrace your adoring fans.

SAGE ADVICE

Social Media Trends in Government

What trends will materialize for social media in government in the near term? An article by David Armano in the *Harvard Business Review* outlines six key social media trends he sees on the horizon:

a. **Social media will become less social.** Too much of a good thing is not a good thing. People will begin paring back their social media interactions, focusing on those delivering the ***greatest*** value.

b. **Corporations will scale up.** Companies and government agencies will ramp up their social media tactics, moving beyond advertising to serving customers and constituents. The example provided is Best Buy's @Twelpforce, a customer service group providing tech answers over Twitter.

c. **Organizations will expand social media interactions through the enticements of games and incentives.** The example is Foursquare where people are rewarded for visiting local places frequently (you can even be "mayor" of your favorite restaurant or watering hole if you visit more frequently than others).

d. **Organizations will create more formal social media policies.** As agencies and companies allow and/or adopt social media interaction, policies for its use will become more clearly defined and enforced.

e. **Mobile devices will drive social interaction.** With companies enforcing stronger social media policies and sales of smart phones skyrocketing, employees will turn to mobile devices to get their daily or hourly "fix."

f. **Sharing no longer means email.** With new tools allowing for the broadcast of articles and websites over networks such as Twitter or Facebook, the email distribution list will be out, and the sharing network list will be in.

While government agencies will likely lag behind corporate America in adopting certain aspects of social media, a desire to connect will drive personal behavior, make government workings more transparent, and open up opportunities for vendors to better interact with buyers. [2]

So, social media is here to stay but is continually evolving and refining itself. To stand out from the crowd of emails, tweets, and posting offer cogent, concise, and compelling content. Make yourself the go-to resource for unique and worthwhile reading.

---

[2] http://blogs.hbr.org/cs/2009/11/six_social_media_trends.html

SAGE ADVICE

It's Tuna Time!

It happens but once a year, a time all government sales and business development people anxiously await. It's the time of the year when government buyers go into a frenzy to spend what's left of their money. There's a prevailing fear that if they don't spend it, their budgets will be cut the next year. Rare is the government organization that says at the end of the year, "Hey, we didn't need all of the money in our budget. We're going to give some of it back."

That means as the end of the fiscal year nears, government buyers go into high gear. They scurry about, making sure all of their budgeted money is spent. It's not that they've been sitting around all year waiting for the end of the year. They often just do not know how much money they will have until the eleventh hour. There would be hell to pay if, at the end of the year, they had to tell their bosses that all funds weren't spent because they didn't get around to it. So, the frenzy begins.

David, a high-performing sales colleague called it Tuna Time. "The tuna are running", he would say, "time to make sure your net is in the water". He knew most of his sales would close during the last month, the last week, even the last day of the year. David would go into warp speed during Tuna Time. A whirling dervish he would become, zipping around the office with one portable phone to his ear and another one jangling in his pocket. He put a cardboard box on his desk to elevate his keyboard so he could stand up, and not waste time sitting down. He scheduled no travel, I'm not sure he even went home. He was "on" 24-hours, working the phones like a Wall Street boiler room broker. One eye was on the fax machine, constantly watching for his paperwork to arrive, the other on the clipboard he carried holding several sheets of notes and phone numbers.

David would often go into the last month of the year well behind his sales objective. But, in the eleventh hour, he always came through. His objective would be met, and often he was the one who pulled the rest of the company through to make its objective. It was both nerve-wracking and a thing of beauty.

Not everyone can be a whirling dervish like David, or even want to be. As the dust settled on the close of the year, David would openly wonder how he could avoid the chaos next year. We never saw him do it, and suspect that now, as president of a company that sells to government, he is still declaring, "It's Tuna Time!" as the year closes.

What those who complained (and there were plenty of complainers) did not see about his last-minute heroics was what David had done throughout the year to make sure Tuna Time would be fruitful. Those people on the other end of the line of his phone, make that phones, were not strangers to David. He knew them, and knew them well. He had worked hard through the year to make sure they knew him as well. With exception of his self-imposed moratorium during Tuna Time, he traveled extensively all year long, seizing every opportunity to get to know his prospects. He made it his mission to understand their mission. Then, he would work to figure out a way to help them fulfill their mission using his products. He would ask lots of questions. He knew which prospects were most likely to come up with money at the end of the year. He also understood that, despite his efforts, it was impossible to predict exactly who that would be. He missed sometimes. But occasionally a "bluebird" would come in, an order he had not anticipated.

Had David not laid the groundwork throughout the year, there would have been no pleasant bluebird surprises. There would have been no Tuna Time and no objectives would have been met.

Seven Myths Take-Aways

- Build personal brand recognition – be a rock star.
  - o Define your unique Personal Brand Traits.
  - o Pair your personal brand traits with content.
  - o Cultivate a network of influencers and communicators.
  - o Commit time to spreading the word.
- Pair your brand traits with useable, desirable, worthwhile content.
- Networking builds visibility and credibility.
- Commit time to build your visibility and focus on the arenas that offer the most promise. Not every outlet is worth your time.
- Cold calling yields low results. Relationships you have built by proving the value of **who you are** and **what you have to offer** yield high results.

CHAPTER THREE

MYTH #3: Always go to the top.

FACT #3: Always go where it hurts the most.

[Rick] One beautiful autumn morning in Washington, D.C., I found myself in a private meeting with a Presidential cabinet Secretary. Through a mutual acquaintance, he had expressed interest in a technology solution I was representing. In fact, as we talked at a social event where we first met weeks before, he pointed his finger at me and said with much enthusiasm that he had heard I had a solution to a problem he wanted solved.

I was naturally pleased, but wondered if the follow-up would actually occur. To my surprise, it did. My colleagues and I went into high-gear preparing a briefing for this highly visible leader. When time came for us to meet, I was surprised that no staffers would be involved. I took that as a positive sign--a cabinet secretary wanting a one-on-one with me.

As the meeting progressed, he wrote many notes on the briefing document I provided. He asked good questions, and the meeting went longer than scheduled. (To this day, I regret not asking for a copy of the itinerary on his desk with my name on it, alongside other meetings with top well-known administration officials.) When the meeting concluded, he told me he was very interested and looked forward to getting my solution in front of his Chief Information Officer. He asked for my cell number, my home number, and any other number I had to make sure he could reach me at a moment's notice as they were very, very busy. Of course, I accommodated.

I left the meeting and its most impressive surroundings thinking I was on the road to helping solve a very troublesome problem for the nation. I would be handsomely rewarded in many ways. Now, all I needed to do was be prepared for the CIO's call, which I was sure I would receive soon…maybe even during the upcoming weekend.

Where's the Chief?

He didn't call.

Not over the weekend.

Not during the next week.

Not the following week.

I called him, left a message saying I was following up on the conversations with the Secretary, knew he would be trying to get in touch with me, and just wanted to make sure I was available. Still no call.

I sent him an email. No response.

As luck would have it, I found myself down the hall from the Secretary's office while visiting on another matter. I figured what the heck, I'll see if he'll give me a few moments of time. I had my host for the other meeting introduce me to the Secretary's chief of staff's secretary. She disappeared, and came back about fifteen minutes later and said, "Yes, the Secretary would like to see you, but you'll have only five minutes to talk to him as he walks to his car to go to his next appointment." I waited around, and my time came.

He greeted me warmly, and asked, "How's it going with (insert CIO's nick name)?"

"Well, sir," I gulped, "He's not contacted me."

He was surprised, and said he still had my card with all of my phone numbers in the top left hand drawer of his desk. He said he would make sure I heard from the CIO soon. He went on to say, "There must be some misunderstanding. I'll take care of it."

"Well, that's more like it", I thought. "Now, I'm getting somewhere."

Within a couple of weeks, I was sitting in front of the CIO. As I launched into my presentation, the CIO told me to get to the point quickly. He knew why I was there, and already liked what I was proposing.

Now, I was really getting somewhere.

That was over six years ago...

And the program still has not been activated. In fact, the Secretary and the CIOs have moved on.

Here's the lesson: Even buy-in at the very top does not mean you will find success when dealing with government. You certainly won't succeed without it, but even a top advisor to the President of the United States cannot get an initiative done just because he or she is enthusiastic about it. **You've got to get "buy-in" up and down the ladder!**

To achieve this, it is imperative to know who the players are, what problems they experience, and how your product or service makes each of their lives easier. We call this "pain mapping". It will serve you well if you incorporate the process into your selling approach.

The Pain Mapping Process

In a great book by Keith Eades, entitled The New Solution Selling, he describes something called a "pain chain." It's a way of identifying the various people involved in a sale (both upstream and downstream from your contact) and their associated pain points.

It's a tenet of "consultative selling," a concept we will beat up on in the next chapter (though we still buy in to its general principles). However, we like this piece of the overall approach and have modified it only slightly to better fit government selling. It starts with what Eades refers to as a "key players list."

The Key Players List

The key players list is just as it sounds—a roster of people whose influence in the organization is significant and whose interdependence is high. During your discovery process, you will want to ask questions surrounding the organizational structure and which individuals are touched by the project associated with your sale. Take note that everyone on this list does not have to be a big cheese. Many times, some of the most influential people in the sales process do not carry a prestigious title. Your list must include these individuals as well.

The Pain Map

Once your list is complete, the next step is to identify critical *pain points, fears,* or significant *motivators* for each individual as they relate to the solutions you offer. Remember, pain points and fears are negative consequences associated with an unsolved problem. For an elected official, for example, not fulfilling a highly visible campaign promise might be a pain point. Motivators are things that might move an individual to a better perceived state of being. Achieving a goal that leads to a career promotion for an appointed official might be a motivator (do not underestimate the power of motivators in the government space—other B2B selling systems tend to overlook this and focus mainly on pain points).

Connect the Pieces

The third step in the pain mapping process is to connect pain points and motivators across individuals. You can do this visually to help see the various connections more easily. Once this process is complete, you will have a pretty nice picture of who your key targets should be and what will push their hot button.

A Pain Map Example

For the example illustrated in Figure 1, let's imagine our prospect is the IT Director for a mid-sized municipality. The Mayor of this city is catching grief from the citizenry about the city's overall emergency response capabilities (consider the fears this might create). Response times for the fire department consistently appear below national standards.

Though the Mayor leads the city, the Fire Chief is responsible for addressing this particular issue, so the pain is connected from the Mayor to him. As we delve into root causes of the pain, we see that response times are slow because of dispatching bottlenecks in the 9-1-1 center. This is a challenge for the 9-1-1 Director (so she's connected to the Fire Chief).

Further digging reveals two root causes of slow dispatching:
1) the 9-1-1 software's inability to locate cellular-based callers
2) its inability to track fire/rescue truck locations in real time.

This leads us to the connection with the City IT Director (the prospect) who must deal with an aging dispatch system, along with political ramifications upstream.

Figure 1

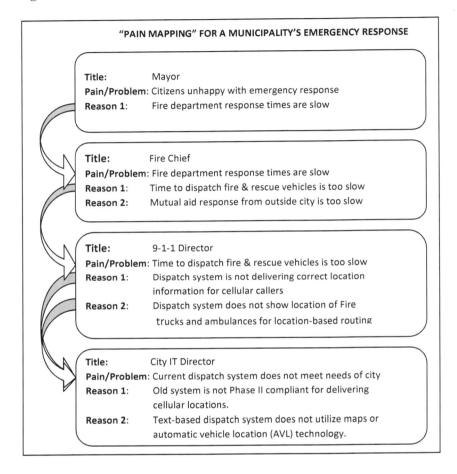

"PAIN MAPPING" FOR A MUNICIPALITY'S EMERGENCY RESPONSE

Title: Mayor
Pain/Problem: Citizens unhappy with emergency response
Reason 1: Fire department response times are slow

Title: Fire Chief
Pain/Problem: Fire department response times are slow
Reason 1: Time to dispatch fire & rescue vehicles is too slow
Reason 2: Mutual aid response from outside city is too slow

Title: 9-1-1 Director
Pain/Problem: Time to dispatch fire & rescue vehicles is too slow
Reason 1: Dispatch system is not delivering correct location information for cellular callers
Reason 2: Dispatch system does not show location of Fire trucks and ambulances for location-based routing

Title: City IT Director
Pain/Problem: Current dispatch system does not meet needs of city
Reason 1: Old system is not Phase II compliant for delivering cellular locations.
Reason 2: Text-based dispatch system does not utilize maps or automatic vehicle location (AVL) technology.

Using the Pain Map

Truly understanding how these problems are interrelated across people and departments can give you excellent insights into how to approach the sale, while helping you identify other allies (or foes) on whom you should be concentrating.

In our emergency response example, you the salesperson could suggest to your IT Director prospect that a meeting with the Fire Chief might be productive. Because no RFP has been issued yet, this should be an appropriate request. The Fire Chief, while not the

Connect the Dots...

Successful sales people are often good at facilitating communications within prospect organizations. You might think communications amongst various sub-groups within an organization (say, a city) would be good...but, they're often not, even though the people involved may see each other on a regular basis and are on good terms. (Often, they aren't.)

We once got points by helping connect the dots between a husband and wife, both managers of public safety organizations within a county, both with a similar problem, both who could benefit from the solution we offered. We guess they had other things to discuss while having dinner with their four young children.

ultimate decision-maker, may be impressed by your solution, creating a strong advocate both across the IT organization and upward to the Mayor's office.

In this case, you didn't "go to the top," but expanded your efforts beyond the immediate prospect, identifying and understanding a key influencer that will certainly help your cause.

You are now ready to formulate a strategy on how to get your story in front of each key player.

Meet My Friend--AIDA

In advertising, there is an acronym used to describe the process for creating successful and persuasive ads. It's called the AIDA model and it consists of the following components:

- Attention
- Interest
- Desire
- Action

Do not let the fact that this model comes from Planet Marketing bother you. This model is applicable for salespeople too. The same steps apply for persuading key players within the sales environment as they do for creating winning advertising campaigns.

The elements of the AIDA model are as follows:

Attention

Our brains are constantly bombarded with inputs and messages. So many, in fact, we learn to subconsciously filter our environment so as not to go completely bananas. This is great for the brain but bad for the salesperson, because **you must capture a prospect's attention before you can do anything else**.

Interest

Assuming you have managed to cut through the cacophony of competing inputs and messages, your work has only just begun. The next challenge is to quickly communicate information that piques the prospect's interest lest they move on to the next distraction.

As a part of the filtering process, our subconscious brains scan the environment looking for things that connect in some way to our perceptions regarding personal safety, conscious or subconscious fears, and emotional attachments. When we feel this connection, we may then focus our attention around the message in order to explore the information in greater detail.

Once the first step of getting a prospect's attention is gained, your job as a salesperson is to **quickly "hit" them with a thought or idea that stimulates their interest**. This makes fertile ground for the next stage.

Desire

Desire, by definition, is the "longing for something that is at the moment beyond reach but may be attainable at some future time."[3] It is an internal tension generated by the realization we do not yet have in our grasp a thing that would provide some perceived physical or emotional benefit.

---

[3] www.dictionary.com.

For salespeople, making a prospect uncomfortable can be profitable. Not through obnoxious or manipulating behavior, but through the ability to create a realization in the prospect's mind that they are missing something important, beneficial or pain-relieving.

Much of what we will discuss throughout this book will give insight on ways to create deeper desire. For now, recognize the fact that there are multiple levels of desire, and your first goal is to **generate enough mental tension to push the sales process forward**.

Don't worry about hurting feelings. Government buyers are generally tough-skinned. They're accustomed to disagreements, pressure, and criticism. They generally want candor more than they want to be made comfortable by a vendor. The more action-oriented they are, the truer this characteristic.

Action

All the desire in the world will not help if you're unable to generate some sort of response or action from the prospect. Of course, the ultimate action is for the prospect to buy what you're selling. However, like desire, there are multiple actions you may need the prospect (or another key player) to take depending on the phase of the sales process.

At first, it may be as simple as persuading the prospect to take your initial call. Later, you may need the prospect to act as a coach (or cheerleader) for other influencers within the organization. (No government sale is made without a coach.) Sometimes, the desired action is no action at all (for example, influencers who may not have the power to make the ultimate decision but sure have the power to mess up your deal.) Whatever the case, action will not occur unless attention, interest and desire have been created beforehand.

Putting Pain Mapping and AIDA Together

Now that you have mapped out the key players and their associated pains, and you also understand the AIDA process of persuasion, you are ready to develop a battle plan for communicating with your prospects and key influencers. *The Key Player Strategy Worksheet* in Figure 2 helps you do just that.

The worksheet allows you to list out each key player, highlight his or her primary pain points or fears, and remind yourself of their "pain map" connections. Further, it allows you to plan for methods to capture each individual's attention, interest and desire. Finally, it provides a place to specify the exact action you'd like for this individual to take.

It should be noted that everything we've discussed here relates to situations where you are selling ahead of the RFP. This is one of the reasons why it is so important to be in front of a prospect long before an official document is released.

Figure 2

KEY PLAYER STRATEGY WORKSHEET

Key Player	Primary Pains/Fears	Connected to:	How will I get his/her attention?	How will I stimulate his/her interest?	How will I create desire for my product?	What specific action do I want him/her to take?
1.						
2.						
3.						
4.						
5.						

SAGE ADVICE

Three Types of Government Buyers

A publication by the General Services Administration (GSA)[4] does a nice job of describing the three types of government buyers within an organization: procurers, influencers and end-users. Understanding the role each one plays is important to successful government marketing.

Procurers are the professionals (often referred to as "contracting officers") charged with managing the purchasing process for any given good or service. They serve as filters and gatekeepers between contractors and program managers or end-users. Procurers are experts in the process details and, depending on the product or service being purchased, generally have insight into appropriate costs/value.

Most of your selling efforts will not be focused here. However, it is important not to forget these key folks. Even though procurers are process experts, they can still benefit from creative or alternative ideas...as long as you follow their rules. They can either be a partner in your sale, or an absolute nightmarish obstacle, depending on how you approach them. Kissing up won't work, but genuine concern for helping them do their job will.

How do you help?

First, understand their pain. They have the difficult job of getting the best value for the organization (not always the cheapest price) while following strict rules. They must satisfy end users, even though they may not fully understand them. They have to deal with the fact that end-users don't understand contracting officers either

---

[4] www.gsa.gov

thus end users are often considered a hindrance, rather than help. (By the way, look for coaches who do not view procurement as an enemy; they're the ones who have figured out how to get what they want by working closely with procurement.)

Secondly, understand procurement rules. They are generally in plain sight. If you don't know the rules, ask. They'll be glad to answer. Finally, remember to constantly demonstrate true value and reliability. That's what procurement people really want. They want stuff they buy to produce success. Otherwise, they have to buy again, do twice as much work the second time, and deal with agitated end users (sometimes who carry guns).

Influencers are the program managers and key decision-makers involved with the purchased product or service. The term "influencer" may seem a bit light as many of these carry considerable, if not near-exclusive, power over decisions. However, the term does reinforce the complex nature of government sales as many stars must align before a contract is signed.

With this group, a first consideration is relieving the pain they're experiencing. If you do not truly understand what it is, keep digging until you do. If they've already published specifications, you may be too late to understand what's behind the written words. But, if you honestly can check the box, then prove you're easy to work with. Reinforce that you know the rules and will not cause headaches. Finally, hammer home you're a safe bet. The more that influencers feel you won't embarrass them down the road, the more likely you'll get the contract.

End-Users are typically specialists in their job. They may not have the broad strategic perspective of a program manager, but they know the details and inner workings of their world better than anyone. That doesn't mean they understand the ins and outs of procurement. They may not. In fact, you may need to help guide them through their own procurement process.

Be wary of the end-user who tells you that you've done a good job, and the decision has been made to buy from you. When you hear this good news, next find out what the real purchasing process will be. The end-user may not know, or may think he knows, but really doesn't know. He may think it's much easier than it really is. How many times have we heard, "All we need to do is take it to bid, and I'm sure you'll do well"? (Then, there was the time I got the green light from an end-user, assumed he was wrong when he said he didn't think procurement would be a difficult process, and received a nice order from him the next day. Who knew?)

Selling messages with the end-user group relates to *features* and *functions* of your solution, but only in a targeted fashion aimed at how these features will resolve pain on a daily basis.

Selling and marketing is most effective when well-targeted. Remember the three types of government buyers, and tailor your approach to each. The payoff is a loyal, long-term client.

Seven Myths Take-Aways

- It is imperative to know who the players are, what problems they experience, and how your product or service makes each of their lives easier.
  - o Get buy-in up and down the ladder
- Compile a Key Players List.
- Draw a Pain Map and plot the path from pain to resolution.
- Put AIDA to work:
  - o Attention
  - o Interest
  - o Desire
  - o Action
- Prepare a Key Player Strategy using a simple worksheet.

CHAPTER FOUR

MYTH #4: Consultative selling is the most desirable method.

FACT #4: Value Portfolio Selling is more effective (and more realistic).

Ask a salesperson today in virtually any industry if their selling approach is "consultative" in nature, and most of them will say, "Absolutely, yes." The innumerable articles and training seminars produced on the topic have conditioned us to think this is the proper answer to the question. It's certainly better than a response of, "No, I'm actually a manipulative jackass who cares only about my commission check and making the monthly payments on my new ski boat."

However, while admirable in its goal, we find the actual practice of pure consultative selling to be fairly difficult to implement—particularly in the government space.

In this chapter, we will take a look at the challenges of consultative selling methods in the public sector space. We won't throw the concept out entirely. We will, instead, offer a method to better adapt this philosophy to government selling practices.

Consultative Selling Origins

The term "consultative selling" was first coined by *New York Times* bestselling author Linda Richardson in the mid-1970s. Upon introduction, the philosophy was revolutionary in sales circles. Up to that point, selling was all about manipulating buyers—herding them like cattle through a chute until the exhausted prospect finally gives up and purchases something.

The consultative selling philosophy stepped away from this "buyer beware" approach, instead placing the customer in the center of the picture. Consultative salespeople learned to spend time understanding and diagnosing customer pain points and needs. Then, and only then, would the salesperson craft an economically viable solution to solve the prospect's problem.

"*Solution selling*," another common sales term was originally minted by Keith Eades in the late 1980's. His books wrapped a more formalized process around the consultative selling concept, providing a framework for salespeople and sales managers to implement the philosophy.

So how can anyone find fault with placing the customer's needs as the central focus of the selling effort (that's a stretch even for contrarians like us)?

Well, we are certainly not advocating a return to manipulative selling. You couldn't do that in the government space even if you wanted to. The truth is we're old softies when it comes to pain-resolution selling methods in general. However, for government buyers there are some serious potential problems with a purely consultative approach. Let's, examine three significant problems with consultative selling while weaving in where it works best, then focus attention on understanding our unique complementary process we call VP Selling (Value Portfolio Selling).

Problems with Consultative Selling

You Won't Always Get the Chance

The first problem with pure consultative selling to government is actually finding an opportunity to do it. Let us be clear. There is absolutely no better strategy than getting to the prospect first, offering consultative advice and ultimately influencing the requirements of the project. Our whole discussion on building relationships and pain mapping hinges on the ability to do this.

However, it takes tremendous resources to always be there first. In practical terms, we rarely find government-oriented businesses able to sustain and grow over time by *always* being there first. In reality, you *will* find yourself responding to RFPs over which you had little or no influence.

Complete purists in consultative or solution selling would recommend salespeople decline to participate in such a tainted selling process which has already progressed beyond the requirements development stage. While good in theory (and perhaps appropriate for other markets), you'll get really hungry taking that position in the government space. Avoid being late to the show when you can, but don't expect to be at the head of the line all of the time.

"Whiteboard" Solutions Aren't Always the Best Fit

The second potential problem with consultative selling to government relates to the conflict between selling custom solutions versus selling off-the-shelf solutions. The consultative approach works very well when your company has the ability to "whiteboard" solutions—that is, create highly tailored products or services for individual customers. Many government contracts require this, so vendors geared organizationally toward customization may do well. However, what if your company's operations and cost structure are incompatible with creating "one-off" solutions? Selling custom solutions can be highly destructive. Technology companies, for example, may find their development resources siphoned off by demands of a large custom buyer at the expense of developing standard products for the broader market. Entirely new customer support structures may be required to truly meet the needs of a custom client.

When we encounter businesses that are unable to handle this level of customization, we frequently find frustrated consultative government salespeople. They believe whole-heartedly in the philosophy, but their company isn't set up to work that way (despite the fact the company encourages and trains them to practice consultative selling).

Consultative Skills Are Rare

The third problem relates to the skill set of any given sales organization. True consultative selling requires a significant degree of personal strength, confidence, experience and insight. The personality traits and skills required to be a consultant are fairly rare, or those abilities tend to be developed and honed over many years. There are many engaging, knowledgeable salespeople in the world who do not have a strong talent for teasing out "big picture" patterns and connections at a high level, then translating those into "little picture" product or service features and function requirements. This is particularly true for promising, but inexperienced, sales and business development people. While supporting methods exist to fill the gaps in selling capabilities (adding sales engineers to the mix, for example), the result is often something less than consultative in nature, despite the lip service to the philosophy.

The Alternative: VP Selling (Value Portfolio Selling)

It is likely anyone reading this book is familiar with the concept of a stock portfolio. You know, it's that thing you pour money into only to see its value plummet by 30% in 24 months.

It turns out, when making purchase decisions, government buyers go through mental processes very similar to those involved in creating a suitable stock portfolio. Buyers must determine the end goal they want to achieve and their available resources. They must evaluate which options would help them achieve these goals, and they must factor in the amount of risk associated with the choices—just like an investor.

Your Solution: Value Portfolio

In effect, they view your entire solution as a "value portfolio," a set of individual pieces that add up to something of worth. Just like a stock portfolio consists of individual components with names like "stocks," "bonds" and "mutual funds," a government buyer's value portfolio for any given solution consists of individual components with names like "features," "price," "service level," and "company reputation." Let's call these *decision factors*. While the worth (price) of individual stocks and bonds is determined by the market, the worth of decision factors in the value portfolio is determined by buyers' perceptions—their needs and their opinions of vendor performance.

Through the selling process, a buyer forms an impression of each solution set (the whole package offered by you and your competitors), compares value portfolios across competitors, and selects a portfolio displaying the greatest "return" relative to the perceived risks.

Applying the Concept to Selling

"Thanks for the personal finance lesson", you reply, "but how does that relate to government selling?" Let's apply this concept to consultative selling and see where it fills in the gaps.

Remember, we said the absolute best strategy for selling to government is to be inside the prospect's office (and in his "head") before the RFP or RFI is issued. We have discussed ideas for becoming a sales rock star so prospects will initiate this conversation, or at least be open to your advances. Once in front of them, it is your job to:

1) begin fleshing out what their ideal value portfolio looks like
2) plant seeds of new ideas that align with problems your products and services solve (assuming these have not already shown up).

Let's walk through this process using a worksheet we have developed. The worksheet is available to you at no cost by registering on our book website:

www.7sellingmyths.com.

Identifying Requirements, Fears, and Positive Feelings

So how about we begin with a little psychology? No need to lie down on a couch—we are not talking about psychotherapy. We're referring to *buying* psychology and how individuals (or groups) make decisions.

We may think government purchasing is a completely rational, objective process based only on the achievement of measurable end results. This is certainly the goal in government buying where analytical and unemotional procurement processes are designed to minimize personal influences.

However, no matter the situation, buying behavior is still an emotional process. It is rooted firmly and inextricably in:

1) the buyer's individual desire to avoid negative emotions
2) the buyer's desire to foster positive emotions.

The psychological need to avoid negative emotions is particularly powerful.

The Power of Fear

Fear, in particular, is a strong negative emotion and a key driver of human decision making. Fear of failure. Fear of success. Fear of being criticized. Fear of losing one's job. Fear of losing votes. Fear of no one reading your book. The list goes on. It's true for all settings--personal and business--but it's especially true in politically-charged environments. Someone up the government agency food chain can instantly have a really bad day from just a single phone call from the media. This fosters an environment of "playing it safe" across most government entities--basically a fear-reduction strategy.

Prospect fears, in their various forms, are feelings we want to hone in on early in the prospecting process.

Our overall strategy will be to:

- Understand their specific problems and fears
- Determine the relative importance of these problems and fears (all fears are not created equal)
- Acknowledge these fears explicitly (see chapter 5 on sales presentations)
- Build a Value Portfolio by reducing this negative emotion through proof of our ability to minimize any possible undesirable outcomes (fear reduction).

We will assume, for the sake of the following example, that we've been successful in getting a meeting with a prospect, and we are pre-RFP so we are able to probe for initial prospect requirements. Let's think a moment about what prospects are *not* saying (their underlying fears) about their stated objectives and requirements that can ultimately help us in motivating them to buy.

Examining Requirements & Fears

Take the example of a government agency software purchase. In response to a salesperson's effective probing, a prospect might say, "The software must be easy to understand and use." A reasonable requirement, what fear is the prospect trying to avoid with this? What is he or she actually saying? Probably something along the lines of, "If this stuff is too complicated, people all over my agency will whine and complain. Somebody will make a big mistake and blame it on the software's poor usability. The whole thing will blow up, and I'll be criticized as the idiot who supported it." On the positive side, a prospect might feel he will be praised for helping choose a software package that is adored by everyone.

Working through each of the prospect's requirements and assigning core fears and positive feelings will bring insight into how to communicate with him effectively. Look for patterns of these and categorize them into Decision Factor Categories as shown in Figure 3.

Figure 3

Step 1: Prospect Requirements, Fears, Positive Feelings & Decision Factor Categories

Stated Requirements	Unstated Fears & Consequences	Positive Feelings	Decision Factor Category
"I want a low initial price."	I'm afraid I'll exceed my budget and be seen as a poor manager.	We'll be able to acquire the software and I'll be seen as a tough negotiator.	Price
"Low ongoing costs are also critical."	I'm afraid we'll have the money the first year, but we won't have the funds to sustain it. I'll be blamed for wasting resources.	We'll be able to derive benefits from the purchase far into the future since we can afford to sustain it.	Price
"The software we buy must be easy to understand and use."	I'm afraid people will complain about the difficulty in using the software and I'll be criticized.	People will use the software and praise my/our decision.	Feature Fit
"I want good customer support available 24/7."	I'm fearful something will go wrong with the software and we won't get help fixing the issue when we need it.	If problems arise, I won't have to deal with them personally.	Customer Support
"I want an "off the shelf" solution."	I'm fearful a custom software solution will eat up my budget and be too difficult to modify. I'll be criticized for bringing in a "one off" solution that locks us into an aging technology.	The software will be continually updated without the expense of custom work. I won't have to go through more procurement headaches in the future.	Off-the-Shelf Solution
"I want a company that has been in business for a long time."	I'm afraid I'll invest in a company that doesn't have staying power for the long term. We'll be stuck with an obsolete solution and I'll look bad.	The company will likely be around to support and update the software. I'll feel more secure knowing the company has longevity.	Company Experience

Translating Problems into Decision Factors

The second step is to translate the various fears and problems into decision factors and determine weightings for how much influence each factor has on the prospect's choice. For example, categories such as features, price, company reputation, custom versus off-the-shelf, time-to-delivery, etc., are all decision factors. Each of these will most likely not carry the same amount of "weight" in the buyer's mind. You must uncover their importance to the buyer(s) by asking probing questions and confirming what you are hearing.

Figure 4 illustrates how this is achieved.

Figure 4

STEP 2: DECISION FACTORS

	Decision Factors	Decision Factor Priorities (Importance Weights)
1.	*Price*	*15%*
2.	*Feature fit*	*25%*
3.	*Company experience*	*10%*
4.	*Service quality*	*30%*
5.	*Off-the-shelf solution*	*15%*
6.	*Intangibles (Relationship)*	*5%*
	Total (Should Sum to 100%)	**100.00%**

Your, the salesperson, through careful prodding, probing and confirming, has determined six key factors impacting the buying decision. You also made a judgment about the relative importance of each of these dimensions. As you can see, service quality is clearly the most important aspect based on prospect feedback—twice as important as price. Feature fit is a close second.

Throughout this process, you are considering how each of these fit with your company's offerings. And, since you are with the prospect before an RFP is issued, you may even be successful in introducing new decision factors that, through no accident, align with the your product offerings.

Determining Decision Factor Components

Each of these broader categories will be made of smaller pieces—we call them "decision factor *components*." Take price for instance. Price often has several related components potentially including sub factors such as: initial price, support costs, upgrade fees, total cost of ownership, replacement financing costs, and more (even payment terms may be considered here). You must understand how the customer defines price and capture each component of the customer's definition within the Value Portfolio process.

The relative importance of each of these components must also be uncovered. Is the customer more concerned with the initial price than the total cost of ownership over time? How much more so? Do budgets limit them from lease or subscription-based pricing? Understanding this detail is critical to creating a strong value portfolio. While we may never know with precision how important each component is, we can at least come up with theories since we're asking boatloads of questions.

Our conclusions for a software acquisition might resemble Figure 5.

Figure 5

STEP 3: DECISION FACTOR COMPONENTS

1.	Price	Component Priorities
a.	*Initial price*	*80%*
b.	*Support (3 Years)*	*20%*
	Total (Should sum to 100%)	100%

2.	Feature fit	
a.	*Hosted solution*	*25%*
b.	*Solution security*	*20%*
c.	*Ease of use*	*15%*
d.	*Reporting flexibility*	*40%*
	Total (Should sum to 100%)	100%

3.	Company experience	
a.	*Years in business*	*10%*
b.	*Experience with this type of solution*	*80%*
c.	*Reputation in this market segment*	*10%*
	Total (Should sum to 100%)	100%

4.	Service quality	
a.	*24/7 Customer service*	*80%*
b.	*Reputation for bug fixes*	*20%*
	Total (Should sum to 100%)	100%

5.	Off-the-shelf solution	
a.	*COTS solution*	*100%*
	Total (Should sum to 100%)	100%

6.	Intangibles (Relationship)	
a.	*Relationship with sales person*	*90%*
b.	*Relationship with others in company*	*10%*
	Total (Should sum to 100%)	100%

Each decision factor has been broken down into pieces and given an importance weighting. Now we know this is looking suspiciously like math. Thankfully, we've given you a great spreadsheet to do the heavy lifting.

The important thing for you to do is **focus on understanding how the customer defines value** through this process. If you have trouble thinking in terms of "weighting," pretend you have 100 pennies to spread across all categories. Give each category the number of pennies you think it deserves based on its importance until all 100 pennies are gone.

Figure 6

STEP 3: DECISION FACTOR COMPONENTS		STEP 4: EVALUATION			
	Component Priorities	Us	Competitor: A	Competitor: B	Competitor: C
1. Price					
a. Initial price	80%	4	5	3	4
b. Support (3 Years)	20%	3	3	3	3
Weighted average		3.8	4.6	3.0	3.8
2. Feature fit					
a. Hosted solution	25%	5	4	5	3
b. Solution security	20%	4	3	3	1
c. Ease of use	15%	5	4	4	3
d. Reporting flexibility	40%	4	4	5	5
Weighted average		4.4	3.8	4.5	3.4
3. Company experience					
a. Years in business	10%	3	3	3	3
b. Experience with this solution	80%	2	4	5	5
c. Reputation in this market	10%	2	4	4	4
Weighted average		2.1	3.9	4.7	4.7
4. Service quality					
a. 24/7 Customer service	80%	3	3	3	3
b. Reputation for bug fixes	20%	2	3	3	3
Weighted average		2.8	3.0	3.0	3.0
5. Off-the-shelf solution					
a. COTS solution	100%	5	5	2	2
Weighted average		5.0	5.0	2.0	2.0
6. Intangibles (Relationship)					
a. Relationship with sales person	90%	5	4	4	4
b. Relationship--others in company	10%	3	3	3	3
Weighted average		4.8	3.9	3.9	3.9

EVALUATION SCALE:

Greatly underperforms competition		Equals the Competition		Greatly outperforms competition
1	2	3	4	5

So, now that we have explored the prospect's decision factors, decision factor components, and their relative importance, we need to evaluate how well we perform on each of these factors. We need to determine how well we stack up against our known competitors.

Figure 6 details this evaluation step. For each of the decision factor components, we can rate our company's products and services using a 1 to 5 scale where 1 is "Greatly underperforms the competition", 3 is "Equals the Competition", and 5 is "Greatly outperforms the competition."

Figure 7 illustrates the last step, calculating Value Portfolio scores for ourselves and the competition. This step takes into account the various decision factors, importance to the customer, and our company's estimated performance on each, and combines them into a single measure that indicates how customers will perceive the total value of our offering.

Figure 7

STEP 5: PORTFOLIO VALUE CALCULATION

	Factor Priority Weighting	Us	Competitor: A	Competitor: B	Competitor: C
1. Price	15%	3.8	4.6	3.0	3.8
2. Feature fit	25%	4.4	3.8	4.5	3.4
3. Company experience	10%	2.1	3.9	4.7	4.7
4. Service quality	30%	2.8	3.0	3.0	3.0
5. Off-the-shelf solution	15%	5.0	5.0	2.0	2.0
6. Intangibles (Relationship)	5%	4.8	3.9	3.9	3.9
Total Portfolio Value Score		3.7	3.9	3.4	3.3

As you can see from this, our overall score is a 3.7—not bad compared to our estimate of where the competition stands. However, Competitor A has a slightly higher total value score, indicating they will be our key opponent. The darker gray highlighted cells illustrate where our rating falls below the competitive field. In this case, our company experience and perceived service quality are areas we must bolster customer perceptions if we are to move ahead of the pack. On the bright side, we are the leader on "feature fit" and tied for the leader on our ability to offer a non-custom "off the shelf" solution.

Sales strategies and tools must be developed to help prop up weakness while highlighting strengths. For example, our lower rating on company experience may be a result of our lack of background working with that particular type of organization. So we might develop a case study that highlights our experience with the general challenges faced by similar customers, even if it's not an exact match. For addressing service quality shortfalls, compiling letters and emails from a few of our existing customers may be just the thing to combat any negative perception issues.

VP Selling When You're Not There First

VP Selling works great when we are the first to ask many of the required questions. But what about situations where we discover the opportunity through a RFP process and all of the requirements are already defined?

VP Selling works there, too, though you may have less ability to influence new decision factors. In fact, many customer procurement teams follow the basic concepts underlying VP Selling in their selection process. They may even spell out some of the details for you. It is not uncommon for RFPs to describe decision factors and importance weightings.

The real trick with RFPs is seeing the bigger picture. When you are first in the prospect's office, your job in the VP Selling process is to help define the value portfolio. However, when analyzing an RFP which you have not influenced, your job in VP Selling is to *reconstruct* the value proposition typically outlined in great detail.

In an RFP, value has been "exploded" into many pieces, parts and descriptions. You must put it back together and understand what is really driving the value. VP Selling helps you do that as well by following the same process just described in gory detail.

VP Selling, overall, is a way to delve into customer "hot button" issues, consider relative importance, and analyze how your offering stacks up against the competition. By focusing on the elements that drive value instead of throwing spaghetti on the wall, you will increase your ability to build a strong value portfolio in the minds of the prospect. You will win more deals.

For those of you who simply can't get enough of our "portfolio" analogy, please enjoy the following:

Figure 8

COMPARISON OF A FINANCIAL PORTFOLIO TO A "VALUE PORTFOLIO"

Financial Portfolio	Value Portfolio
Asset Category → (e.g. Small Cap, International, Large Cap)	**Decision Factor** (e.g. Ease of Use, Price, Security)
Asset Allocation Strategy → (How much is allocated to each asset category?)	**Decision Factor Priorities** (What is the relative importance of each decision factor?)
Investment Vehicle → (e.g. Stock, Bond, Mutual Fund)	**Product Feature** (SQL database, hosted solution, calls per hour)
Return on Investment → (e.g. average yield over 10 years) (Does it perform as desired/expected?)	**Feature Performance** (Does the product offer the feature?)
Beta → (How volatile (risky) is a stock compared to others in the market?)	**Feature Performance Risk** (How much risk is there that the feature will not meet my needs?)
Portfolio Risk → (How much risk am I assuming with this combination of assets?)	**Provider Risk** (How much risk am I assuming with this particular vendor?)

SAGE ADVICE

Will Government RFPs Soon be Extinct?

In his keynote address at the 2009 Health IT Conference in Washington, Aneesh Chopra, Federal Chief Technology Officer, discussed how the current RFP model, originally created to provide fairness in procuring commodity products, does not fit well with complex technology acquisitions such as information systems and services.

Chopra said he intends to seek a different approach to acquire health and other IT-related systems with tools such as www.DefenseSolutions.gov– a web-site touted as a "new ideas portal." The site outlines DoD problems by categorized "themes" and seeks vendor input on possible solutions. It also promises to deliver initial feedback on proposed ideas within 30 days.

We believe this new way of thinking could provide positive results if it can be fully executed. Though it is unlikely RFPs are going the way of the Dodo bird anytime soon, such a non-traditional acquisition approach certainly taps into America's greatest asset–it's creative and assertive people.

Seven Myths Take-Aways

- Consultative selling works best when you are at the head of the line, when you are there at the beginning to influence and guide the projects requirements and parameters.

- Consultative selling works well when tailoring custom solutions, not off-the-shelf products or services.

- Value portfolio selling allows prospects to see your entire solution(s) as a set of individual pieces that add up to something of worth.

- The steps in Value Portfolio Selling are:

    o Identify requirements, fears, and positive feelings.

    o Examine and rate those requirements, fears, and feelings.

    o Translate them into decision factors.

    o Focus on how the customer defines value.

    o Match your offerings to those values.

CHAPTER FIVE

MYTH #5: Sales presentations really seal the deal.

FACT #5: They're not that important and you're probably doing them wrong anyway.

Sales presentations are frequently considered the lifeblood of successful selling. The slickest pitch wins after all, right? Certainly delivering a smooth, polished presentation is preferred over stammering and bumbling one's way through a slide deck. In government selling, however, a solid presentation will not necessarily seal the deal.

Most presentations are geared for the convenience of the salesperson instead of the listener. Even the most entertaining and engaging presenters can make costly mistakes structuring content.

Let's carefully examine the sales presentation and uncover effective secrets to clearly presenting value. We'll look at why presentations are overrated, then compare and contrast the "typical" sales presentation with our problem resolution method, giving you an automatic edge over those pesky competitors.

Not That Important?

Once again your authors have crossed a sacred line of sales doctrine into blasphemous irreverence. Oh, the heresy of suggesting sales presentations are not that important. How can this be? Well, we are not suggesting presentations are NEVER important. We've seen our share of government deals where the presentation seemed to make or break the sale.

In the grand scheme of things, however, other elements of the sale are typically much more crucial. For example, without a strong written proposal, you will likely never get a chance to give a face-to-face presentation (often, a selection committee will select only a few vendors to give presentations from a much larger pool of proposals).

In our experience and study of government buying behaviors, we often find that clear preferences are already formed prior to the presentation meeting. As hard as they may try, buyers do not come into a presentation with a completely "blank slate." Instead, they are subconsciously looking for signals that either support or disconfirm their predisposed notions. It does not mean a firm decision has been made, and it does not mean you can't blow the lead position by giving a poor presentation. You can. It just means other factors can be more important.

So why focus on it at all? Knowing a presentation can be a tipping point for success or failure when the competition is close, it makes sense to try to gain every competitive advantage during this step. Because presentations are often so poorly given, it means you have the chance to be a real standout by using methods discussed here. First, let's examine the usual way of giving sales presentations. Then we'll see why there is room for much improvement.

The Typical Approach

Sales warriors often enter the battlefield armed with a Microsoft PowerPoint® presentation or a stack of handout of materials. The sales person begins the session with a historical timeline of company history. Perhaps his/her experience with the organization is highlighted. Then, the demo begins. For the next 45 minutes, prospects are barraged with product details, specifications, features and functions. Slides are crammed with words and diagrams as if white-space was the enemy of prospect clarity--a blight to be eradicated at all costs. Along the way, the presenter stresses key points he or she believes to be competitive advantages (reading verbatim from the bullet points to make sure nothing is missed, of course). After exhausting every possible product element, the presenter finishes the formal presentation with pricing information, followed by questions from the floor.

Sound familiar? We have all witnessed these types of proceedings, and most likely we are all guilty of delivering presentations like this. Yet this is not the most effective way of delivering compelling information to prospects. What are the key elements of a successful sales presentation? Let's examine a few secrets to improving prospect understanding and retention.

Presentation Flow (A.K.A.—The "Freebird" Strategy)

If you have ever seen a concert given by legendary acts like The Rolling Stones, or perennial southern rock gods Lynyrd Skynyrd, you know a great deal about proper presentation flow. How so? Well, let's think about the way these exciting live-entertainment events are put together for maximum audience impact.

First, the house lights are darkened and tension-building music creates drama and suspense. With a blast of lights, smoke, and sparks, the show begins with a high-energy, classic song everyone knows. The crowd goes wild as the anticipation ends and the experience of hearing original artists deliver one of their old-time favorites begins. The next few songs are also recognizable standards in order to keep the crowd invigorated.

At some point during the show the band will introduce new music from their latest record (often a good time to hit the snack bar). The act may also find a time to "slow it down a bit" with a ballad, giving concert-goers the chance to transform their individual cell phones into a sea of twinkling lights. (I remember when it was cigarette lighters). Nice, but truthfully not what everyone came to see. Somewhere during the course of a familiar song, the lead singer will stop and point the microphone at the audience. Powerful lights may illuminate the arena as a cue for the audience to take over singing duties and engage in direct participation with the event. The evening continues to take its musical course.

As the show draws to an end, the band will perform one last emotionally-charged number, finishing with a flurry of lights, pyrotechnics and a sincere, "We love you Cleveland." But, wait...is it really over? They didn't play THE song. Did they forget? Did you miss it somehow when you went for a chili dog and cheese pretzel? Not likely. The lights remain low until the crowd begins to chant and clap in unison. Just as the crowd noise rises to a fever pitch, the spotlights explode again and the band members return to the stage for one last song--the ENCORE.

The first few notes are played, and you sigh with relief; Ah, "Freebird." Finally.

Now your quest is over and your musical thirst is quenched. Still on a high of endorphins (and whatever else was wafting around the arena) you barely notice the gridlock in the parking lot as you exit with all your dreams and expectations completely fulfilled. And, guess what, that "Freebird" high probably prompts you to buy a $35 tee-shirt that cost the band a few bucks. (Hmm, nothing "free" about that.)

OK. So your next sales presentation may not have all the appeal and exhilaration of a classic rock concert, there are a few things we can learn from this experience. First, let's talk about how presentations should be structured—that is, the order of topics. Changing the content sequence to mirror the flow of a concert will often automatically generate a greater positive psychological impact.

To understand why, we must understand the concepts of "primacy" and "recency." In a nutshell, memory researchers have discovered people have a tendency to better recall information that is presented first and last in a sequence. For example, when given a moderately lengthy list of words, research subjects are more likely to remember the first few and the last few in a sequence than those presented in the middle. [5] This is referred to as the "serial position effect."

How does this relate to sales presentations? It suggests we should place the really "good stuff" first and last in the presentation, and bury the necessary-but-not-so-good-stuff in the middle.

For example, examine the following presentation outline for a company with impressive, relevant customer references and a strong company history as an innovator:

- Salesperson's brief introduction and thanks (The house lights go down).
- Power list of customer references and satisfied customer quotes (The explosive opening song).
- Problem, Cause, Solution, Benefit section (The hits keep coming).
- Pause for questions from the floor (Audience participation).
- Pricing (Songs from the new album).
- Contractual arrangements and service level agreements (The ballads).
- Impressive company history points (The "almost" final number).
- Customer(s) case study tying it all together (The heart-stopping finale).

Note the key differences between this approach and the typical sales presentation. In the typical approach, a salesperson might start off well enough by introducing the company and a bit of history. Frequently this is more of a warm-up act than a powerful opening number. Generally there is a rush to get to the demo

---

[5] Kohler, Christine. "Order Effects Theory : Primacy versus Recency". Center for Interactive Advertising, The University of Texas at Austin.

section because that's the place where the presenter is most comfortable (and where the slides have lots of words or pictures on them).

Pricing is often saved until the very end. The theory behind this is a salesperson is building up audience value perceptions *before* costs are discussed. Though this is true to a point, we believe it is a mistake to make pricing information the encore—the last thing the audience experiences…or remembers. Unless this is a monster competitive advantage and you are positioning yourself as an industry-wide low-cost provider, you will end your "concert" with a downer of a slow song. We are not saying that placing presentation items such as pricing in the middle will magically keep prospects from revisiting the topic and/or ripping your head off if required. From our understanding of primacy and recency concepts, and because we learned our lessons the hard way, we now believe that ending with other strong points will help reduce the fixation on price and emphasize other more emotionally rewarding elements.

Problem, Cause, Solution, Benefit

In addition to presentation structure problems, sales demos are often inadequate because they force prospects to do the mental work in making connections between demo features and their own needs or pains. Our goal as salespeople should be to make these connections crystal clear in the prospect's mind requiring very little effort on their part.

For the salesperson familiar with their product, it seems obvious as to how or why a given feature would be helpful. Simply illustrating the feature should hit a mental nerve and create connections to prospect problems, right? This can happen, but why create all the mental gymnastics? The approach is backwards. Instead, salespeople should illustrate their grasp of individual prospect pain points, and then describe how the features of their product or service make the pain go away. This aligns with the Value-Portfolio Selling process we discussed in the previous chapter. You are really just walking through the prospect-defined components of value, then showing how your solution helps.

To achieve this, we recommend the "meat" of presentations follow this order:

- Problem (Fear)
- Cause
- Solution
- Benefit

We'll take a closer look at each of these elements to better understand how to incorporate them into successful presentations. Let's use a more specific example. Let's assume our prospect is looking for an asset tracking software package.

Problem

"Problem" is a specific challenge or barrier that makes a prospect's life difficult or keeps him from achieving a desired goal. Remember, the root of this is fear, as we defined in our VP Selling model. The concept of "selling to the pain" is not a new one. Nevertheless, salespeople rarely structure their presentation specifically around prospect fears, challenges and pain points. Generally the focus centers on product features. Effective salespeople make attempts to tie features to pain, and ineffective ones hope the prospect will figure it out on their own from the proposal document. Great ones leave the prospect with the feeling the salesperson really "gets it."

Cause

"Cause" is the reason why there is a problem in the first place. There may be multiple causes related to a single problem. Verbalizing why the problem exists shows you've done your homework and you really understand the prospect's challenges— not just selling a canned solution. At times, the cause is obvious and requires little detailed description. Other times, the cause is complex and requires a deeper analysis. Either way, the cause should at least be addressed.

Solution

This is where you and your product shine. Here, you underscore how what you offer addresses root causes and solves the specific problem. Also, this is where you want to hammer home any unique selling advantages your competition cannot easily replicate.

Benefit

Don't stop at presenting a description of the solution. Wrap up each problem-solution with a description of the *benefits* the prospect will receive in solving them. There are two main components of this; emotional and rational.

On the emotional side, this is a great place to illustrate how fears, identified in our VP Selling approach, dissipate by deploying your solution. Illustrate specifically how purchasing your product or service will diminish negative emotions and heighten positive ones. Government buyers may seem staid and stiff at first, but they are just as responsive, perhaps even more, than other buyers to diminished negative emotions and heightened positive ones. Do be careful, though. Too many "rainbows and butterflies" could sound hokey, so practice caution and be smart.

On the rational side, this is the place to bring out the analytical guns. If you have strong historical return on investment statistics or quantifiable cost saving studies across your customer base, now is the time to let this fly. It will be the icing on the proverbial cake.

The graphic in Figure 9 shows how this might come together on a slide. Where possible, each slide illustrates a specific unique advantage. Further, the slide highlights the problem/cause (combined in this case), the solution to ease the pain, and the overall benefits. Notice the benefits cover both emotional and rational elements.

By carefully choosing words, all of this can happen effectively in a relatively small amount of space.

Figure 9

Unique Advantage: Redundancy

- **Problem & Cause:**
  With no backup, agency systems can fail when you need them most.

- **Solution:** Product XYZ is built to offer:
  - On-site redundancy
    - Connected on-premise servers
    - Automatic failover
  - Geographic redundancy
    - Geographically separated backup servers
    - Instant switchover

- **Benefits:**
  - It works every time you need it.
  - 20% lower maintenance costs.
  - Peace of mind.

The Slide Presentation

A few of you are fortunate enough to have the support of a crack marketing department capable of creating hypnotically beautiful sales presentations, complete with celebrity endorsements and 3-D multimedia product demonstrations, directed by James Cameron and narrated by James Earl Jones. Many of you, due to the need to customize your pitch, will receive a standard corporate template to fill-in and modify according to your needs. And some of you will be using a hand-me-down slide deck, originally created when Lynard Skynard was playing wedding receptions and Bill Gates was wearing braces.

In all but the rarest of cases, you as a salesperson will have a great deal of impact on the look and feel of your slide presentation. You always have final edit rights since you're the one giving it. If you're practicing VP Selling, canned presentations simply won't do. You'll need to tailor the information to the prospect's value drivers.

While turning you into a graphic design expert is beyond the scope of this book, there are some basics to think about when developing a presentation. Other things are more important in the grand scheme of things, however, you might as well do everything in your power to tip the scales in your favor—including ensuring your presentation is a notch above the rest.

Document or Presentation?

When considering presentation aesthetics, one question to ask yourself is, "Will my slides only be used as an aid to the presentation, or will they be an important leave-behind document?"

If the slides are strictly to be used as supporting visuals for a verbal demonstration, you should focus on strong images and diagrams to help tell your story. (We will discuss word pictures in the following pages.) Words themselves should be sparse. Studies have shown that verbal retention is enhanced most when the listener is presented a single, large image that relates to what the speaker is saying.

If the slide presentation will become a key sales document to which prospects will refer later, then you will need to beef up the verbiage a bit. A bright yellow happy face on a slide may make a great accompaniment to what you are saying, but two weeks later, when the purchasing team is reviewing presentations, they'll be perplexed (though perhaps mildly entertained). Provide the audience with enough written content to allow the presentation to stand on its own.

It is critical to remember that different people have different personal preferences about receiving information. Some may like charts and graphs. Others gloss over them. Lorin likes to explain them in a presentation. Rick likes to show them, move on, and hope no one asks questions about them.

[Rick] I'll never forget a presentation I did for a group of mostly engineers. I placed all types of engineering-type charts in the presentation, thinking they would like that. But, the only slide they asked me to go back to was an "effect" slide I had inserted (and glossed over) that showed rocks lined up in a pool of water. They wanted to discuss the symbolism of the slide. The senior official, an engineer himself, said it was the best presentation he had ever seen. (Imagine that!)

Too Many Words

One of the most common presentation errors salespeople make is cramming too many words on a slide. Everyone knows it's a mistake. Everyone does it anyway, particularly in government.

For some, the problem stems from a lack of confidence—a fear that some key point will be missed or an important feature will be described inaccurately. For others, it's basic laziness or a lack of preparation. Slides become a crutch for those unwilling or unable to spend the time rehearsing and polishing the pitch or a crutch for not truly understanding the nature of the pain they are trying to relieve or how they can do it. If you lack understanding, you may be just throwing a bunch of spaghetti against the wall to see what sticks. Sorry, the government sales walls are very slippery.

Whatever the reason, filling the screen with words is not good. Even in situations where presentation slides will be used as a reference document, words should be chosen carefully. Every word must fight for its right to exist on the page. You may need one sentence to provide clear context or introduce a concept, but most bullet points should consist of only a few words. Show only three to five main points per slide. If you need more room, create another slide.

In all honesty, we know this can be a real challenge, especially when following our advice on presenting pain, cause, solution and benefits. It's a lot of ground to cover for one slide. While this information can be split across multiple slides, we tend to like it on one. With a little word-wrangling, you should be able to condense your message and still make it fit. Refer back to Figure 9 as an example of a slide that pulls all of the elements together without too much white space erosion.

Animations & Transitions

Unless you're creating a commercial for a monster truck rally, you should keep the animations (movement of pictures or text) and transitions (what happens when one slide changes to another) to a bare minimum. Just because MS PowerPoint® is capable of doing something does not mean you *should* do it. No one wants to see your slide build one letter at a time or fly in like confetti in a wind storm. It's distracting and will hinder your message from getting through to the audience. Besides, it's just not cool anymore. Even fifth graders don't use those effects these days.

Restrained and tasteful use of animations can be effective. For example, the "Fade" animation option presents a polished way to introduce information on the slide. When dealing with a larger blocks of text, allow your bullet points to: 1) enter the screen one thought at a time, and 2) fade to gray as the next item is introduced. This nifty trick keeps the audience from being overwhelmed with too much information at once.[6]

Likewise, the use of transitions should be limited. "Fade Smoothly" or "Fade Through Black" options are best. These will give you a clean, professional look without major distraction.

Though you will not hear us say it often, sometimes less is more. With animations and transitions, it's absolutely true.

---

[6] It's the "After Animate" function. Check out
http://presentationsoft.about.com/od/powerpointtips/ss/080124dimtext.htm

Notes

Still worried you'll forget something important because it's not on the slide? Consider using the notes section within the presentation. You can input any text there that will remind you of your most important points, then use MS PowerPoint®'s dual monitor mode (also called "Presenter's View"). This feature will allow you to view your notes and slides together on a laptop, while the audience only sees the slides projected onto a screen or second monitor (see Figure 10).

Another use for the notes section relates to the "document versus presentation" discussion. When your presentation will also serve as a stand-alone document, you can utilize the notes section to add verbiage that would otherwise be too lengthy for the slide itself. This allows you to have the best of both worlds; slides that are streamlined and well summarized, and text that provides deeper descriptions and greater detail.

Audiences can view these notes within the presentation file later, or you can print out handouts for them which will show both the slides and the notes (see Figure 11).[7]

Just make sure you are cautious about what you place into the notes field. Silly comments, or personal notes intended only for the presenter, could unintentionally find their way to audience members after the fact. Don't forget you have added them to the file. Also, notes should be used as an aid, not a crutch. Notes should not be used as a verbatim script. Reading these to the audience is really no better than reading points on a slide. Instead, place key words within the notes section to spark your memory, then prepare and rehearse for a smooth delivery.

---

[7] Look up "Create and Print Handouts" in MS PowerPoint help.

Figure 10

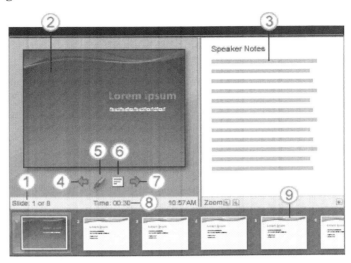

1 The slide number (for example, slide 1 of an 8-slide presentation)

2 The slide you are currently showing to the audience

3 The speaker's notes, which you can use as a script for your presentation

4 Click to go to the previous slide

5 The pen or higlighter

6 Click to display a menu that enables you to end the show, darken or lighten the audience screen,

7 Click to go to the next slide

8 The elapsed time of your presentation, in hours and minutes

9 Slide thumbnails that you can click to skip a slide or to return to a slide that you already presented

Figure 11

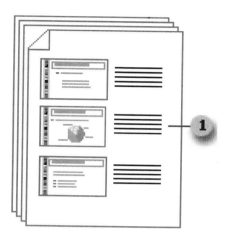

1 The three-slides-per-page handout includes lined space for note taking by the audience.

FIGURE 10 & 11 SOURCE: MS PowerPoint Help (2007)

Images as Word Pictures

The use of images within presentations can help keep audiences engaged and aid in retention of your message. Many presentations, however, fall short in the visual department, relying on cheesy clip art or no pictures at all.

Ideally, your images should provide a clear tie-in to the message of the slide. That's not to say the image must replicate precisely the main idea. Conceptual images that portray a metaphor or symbol of the main point have proven to impact audiences more than simple visual reproductions.

For example, look again at the slide in Figure 9. You will notice the image of a businessman falling into a net—a metaphorical "backup plan" in case something goes wrong. This connects the benefit message of "peace of mind" and "reliability."

It would have been just as easy to show an image of two computers or servers, but the result would be less visually interesting and less impacting. There is something about the audience "working through" the connection of the image to the message that helps them better learn and retain information.

Notice, too, this is an actual picture—not a cartoonish illustration graphic. Real pictures are much preferred over the standard clip art files available in Microsoft and other products. These better-quality images add a level of professionalism not achievable with simple clip art (Microsoft now offers a variety of royalty-free images online for use in their products).

Whatever you do, please promise us one thing: you will never, ever use this guy in your presentations:

If we can save just one salesperson from the tragic effects of Screen Bean® man, it will have been worth all the effort.

Diagrams

Diagrams are frequently required in government selling presentations. While a diagram is supposed to be an aid to learning, most of them end up looking like a schematic for a nuclear reactor (not a problem if you're selling nuclear reactors, I suppose). Text and icons become too small for recognition and the whole thing becomes more obstacle than aid.

While diagrams are designed to simplify and summarize, the answer to better clarity may actually be to *add* more presentation content. Here are some steps to making diagrams more functional:

Start with the highest level. One of the problems with diagrams is the audience is hit with every level of detail at once. This can be overwhelming and confusing. Alternatively, examine your diagram and define the main "branches" or critical paths. Remove the other paths and labels for now and make this your first slide. This will give audience members a conceptual overview of the process you are describing without getting into the weeds too quickly.

Zoom in on each branch individually. Now that audience members have an overall idea where you're going with the diagram, create individual slides for each major branch in the process. You have sufficient room to add details and labels to at a lower level for better clarity. Paths leading to other major branches not covered on the slide can be represented by a dotted line and a shape or icon labeled with the name of the branch.

Consider adding navigation. Many times, diagrams will be a catalyst for generating discussion between a presenter and the audience. As such, there is frequently a need to jump back and forth between branches of the process as the interaction unfolds. MS PowerPoint® will allow you to insert hyperlinks and navigation buttons into your slides to make this easier.[8]

By doing this, you can easily "drill" into the key branches then return to the diagram overview "home." It makes for an impressive demonstration and provides participants a way to refresh their memory once the presentation is over, and you have provided the slides as a computer file.

Contact Information Slide

Remember to add a slide at the end of your presentation with full contact information details. Include at a minimum:

- Your name
- Organization

---

[8] Lookup "Insert a Hyperlink" in MS PowerPoint Help for more details.

- Email address
- Office phone
- Mobile Phone
- Company website

Many times presentation files live on long after a deal is over. Having contact information integrated into the slide presentation provides a means for audience members to contact you in the future with little effort. Even deals that are lost may later resurface in the form of a prospect unhappy with a purchase from a competitor, reaching out to you looking for a replacement solution. They just might remember your dazzling presentation and want you to ride back in and save the day.

SAGE ADVICE

The Presentation Shoot Out

We've earned our stripes in selling to the government partly because we've found ourselves on both sides of the table. We've spent more than our share of time on the "pitch" side, working hard to help government agencies decide to do business with us. And, we've found ourselves on the "catch" side, working hard to help government agencies decide to do business with other vendors. Now, that's not because we work hard for our competitors. It's because we were hired by the government to help make buying decisions. It's an interesting place to be.

Recently as catchers, we were asked to help a state agency choose a software vendor from a very competitive market place. We narrowed the finalists to four, and then watched as the games began. The dreaded shoot-out day was scheduled. Each vendor was given an hour to show their stuff. They were all well prepared. They all knew what the customer's hot buttons were. They all knew who their competition was. They all had strong solutions with strong feature sets. They all had a shot at winning the business. Shoot-out day was to be a game-changer, a time for the vendors to stand out. So, who stood out? See if you can decide.

Vendor Number One: One person showed up, a young fellow. Although he had been told who would be in the room, he asked everyone to introduce themselves. He had been told what they wanted to hear, but he sat down at a table (instead of using the podium) and asked a batch of questions that we had previously answered. Then, he went rapid fire through his presentation and demonstration, occasionally stopping for a question or two. He finished a bit ahead of time.

Vendor Number Two: Showed up with five representatives, two of them local. The presenter did a fine job connecting the dots between the customer's needs and the company's solution. His sales engineer was on-hand driving the demo, for the most part keeping up with the fast-pace. All five of the company's representatives participated in the dialogue.

Vendor Number Three: An impressive presenter, the President of her company. Her presentation was slick and she showed not only a strong feature set, but new things in development she thought would interest the customer. She dropped impressive names.

Vendor Number Four: He immediately established credibility by stating he had worked in the agency's profession of law enforcement. He answered very quickly on his feet when challenged. "Why did you stop being a cop? Were you indicted?" the crusty Major asked with a smirk. "No, I left to follow my true love to another state", the presenter answered. Even the Major was impressed. The presentation was smooth and genuine. Although his customer interface wasn't real cool, his demo showed a feature-rich solution

Now, which of these stood out? Think about it a bit. Number One asked good questions and was proficient at his presentation and demo. Number Two came in force and showed a good understanding of the customer. Number Three demonstrated strong commitment by the president and a good product road map. Number Four really connected to the audience.

Not a simple selection, is it? Can't decide? Well, neither could the customer.

After the last vendor left, the customer team said all presentations were good, but none of them stood out. They said they saw very little that would help them make their decision. (Fortunately, they had a good consultant to help them figure it out.)

You see, it's tough to stand out in a vendor shoot out...almost impossible. Your best bet is to make your prospects love you so much that they won't find a shoot-out necessary. (Yes, this is possible. Read the rest of the book.) If you find yourself in a shoot-out, you'd best not count on standing out in a presentation. At the same time, you'd best not blow it...or you'll find yourself standing out in a way you hadn't hoped. Even if a good presentation doesn't win a sale, a bad one can certainly lose one.

Here are some lessons from each of the presentations:

Vendor Number One: Even though the presenter's questions had been answered ahead of time, the customers were impressed. They didn't tell him anything he didn't already know, but they liked being asked. It made them more confident that what was to follow would address their needs.

Vendor Number Two: Despite having an excellent presenter, the break-down in communications between the presenter and the engineer driving the demo cost them. The customers noticed and privately complained about it. They said the presentation was confusing, made worse by the fact that several of the company representatives started talking at once. We are pretty sure they were trying to help out their struggling colleague in the front of the room. But, they didn't. The presenter never regained control.

If you're going in as a team for a presentation, make sure everyone knows their role in advance. Whoever is in the front of the room should keep control of the presentation. If you do not trust him to steer, don't give him the wheel! Rehearse as a team. Then, rehearse some more.

During the presentation, non-presenting team members should show support for the presenter. Give the guy up front a discreet encouraging smile or thumbs up. And, if he gets a frog in his throat, get him some water! **[(*Rick*) OK, a sensitive subject. I went through a grueling all day Sunday pre-presentation session once where seven people spent the day telling me what to say rather than listening to what I had planned to say, which turned out to be the same thing. (We should have spent the time rehearsing.) The next morning? More of the same. That afternoon during the presentation, I got a frog in my throat and was hoarse. I needed a**

SEVEN MYTHS OF SELLING TO GOVERNMENT

drink of water. I thought one of my colleagues would notice, and come to my rescue. I did everything I could think of just short of stopping the presentation and asking one of them to fetch me some water. My colleagues missed every clue. I worked through it and the presentation was well-received. However, I'm still touchy about the whole ordeal (as you can tell.). Folks, if you're in the back of the room, do the guy in the front of the room a favor and show him some support. Heck, do it for yourself. The better he looks up front, the better you look.]

Vendor Number Three: Bringing out the big guns can be a winning strategy if deployed at the right time. On one hand, it illustrates commitment to the customer at the highest levels of the organization. On the other, depending on what is being sold, relying on the company President to deliver the bulk of a presentation may raise questions as to whether the company is sizable enough to really meet customer needs.

Vendor Number Four: He did a fine job, but these days, if the user experience appears weak, the presentation is weak. Not much he could have done about that. However, because he established a rapport with the audience, the private customer post-mortem was kind to him.

Seven Myths Take-Aways

- Structure your presentations like this:
  - Brief intro and thanks
  - Power list of customer references
  - Problem, cause, solution, benefits
  - Questions from the floor
  - Pricing
  - Contractual arrangements and service level agreements
  - Impressive company history points
  - Customer case studies
- The meat of a presentation should be
  - Problem (fear)
  - Cause
  - Solution
  - Benefit

CHAPTER SIX

MYTH #6: Good salespeople overcome objections & close the sale.

FACT #6: Closing & objection handling are way overrated.

Countless books and seminars have been created over the years educating sales people on the fine art of objection-handling and closing. In fact, for in-house sales training, these areas typically receive the majority of attention. Some in the professional selling field will find it total heresy to suggest objection-handling and closing techniques are not viable practices; truthfully, they are ineffective methods in the government procurement process.

The Limitations of Overcoming Objections

Overcoming objections is a "directing" tactic designed to craftily replace negative prospect perceptions with positive ones. As generally taught, it is a method by which we attempt to out-smart and out-maneuver prospects in a tit-for-tat game of cerebral sparring. They raise a concern with the product or service; we squash it like a bug with our silver-tongued response. They attempt to squeeze out of this stranglehold with another reason not to buy; we are ready to tighten the noose with our market research and Microsoft Excel® charts. With all possible excuses exhausted, the dazed prospect is left with nothing to do but pull out his checkbook and buy what we are selling. Sounds nifty, but here's why it doesn't work in government selling:

You may never get the chance to hear objections. The government procurement process is built to minimize prospect manipulation. You may never get the opportunity to play the objection-handling game when dealing with government buyers. Your story must often be told almost completely through proposal documents and/or presentations. While questions may arise at points during customer interaction, your best hope is to provide solid answers. Rarely can you direct the process this much.

You cannot anticipate every objection. Traditional objection-handling focuses on anticipating objections before the meeting and developing comprehensive answers to common prospect obstacles. While this makes sense to a degree, it is also impossible to predict every path the prospect might take with questions or objections. Salespeople focused on providing the "party line" response to objections may get rattled when presented with an unfamiliar road block.

The objection they are giving may not be the real obstacle. One of the biggest reasons this doesn't work is the fact that prospect's verbalized buying objections are often *not* the real barriers to purchasing. They may be facing job pressures unknown to you. They may have other priorities vying for competing resources. They may be anticipating a role change and just don't want to deal with the decision. This is common in government sales around election time. You may have offended them. Government buyers can be a sensitive lot. Heck, they may just hate your tie or loathe your haircut. These types of factors are seldom stated, yet can be a much bigger barrier to success than their purported objections. Relying solely on the ability to overcome objections often leaves government salespeople frustrated, wondering "what went wrong" in an otherwise perfect execution.

What do we do instead? Before we answer this question, let's examine a second sales technique that receives a great deal of attention in the "books" but has little practical value in government sales—the almighty close.

Limitations of Closing Techniques

Closing is a process by which salespeople push a prospect to uncover (and hopefully eliminate) latent objections, discover where the prospect falls in the buying process, and ultimately and simply "ask for the business." There are trial closes, assumptive closes, shame closes, humor closes…even an approach called the "Golden Bridge Close" which has something to do with Sun Tzu.[9]

Sales managers are often quick to diagnose a salesperson's poor performance as an "inability to close," yet it is likely other factors play a much greater role in their lack of success.

Here is why traditional closing doesn't work in government selling: **You may never get the chance to close a prospect.**

Because of past abuses and a desire to foster competitiveness within government procurement, the process is designed to remove as much "salesmanship" as possible. RFPs are issued publicly. Questions must be asked at an open bidder's conference or through other public means. There is no direct access to decision-makers after a point, but only to an assigned procurement officer. Purchase decisions are documented, published openly, and must hold up under scrutiny. Typically there is a protest process available for

---

[9] For those of you not up on Sino-military history or who have not seen the classic 80's movie *Wall Street*, Sun Tzu was a Chinese military strategist who lived around 600 B.C. He wrote a well-known warfare strategy book entitled The Art of War. The Golden Bridge Close relates to a strategy of leaving your enemy the option for a face-saving retreat, as opposed to leaving no alternative but a full-scale direct conflict to the death. In selling, this supposedly means effectively disparaging all other options except the one you want them to take. The desired alternative is not offered explicitly—instead the prospect believes he/she has made the decision on their own. Now you know.

losing bidders to follow if they do not like the outcome. Try working your Sun Tzu magic on that.

Multiple people involved in buying make closing impossible. Even if you have an opportunity to push for a close with your primary contact, multiple people are almost always involved in making the government buying decision. Most often a purchasing manager will be ultimately responsible for handling the paperwork. You will be at their mercy from a timing standpoint, and you may even hit unanticipated roadblocks that will stall the deal even though the "decision-maker" you have courted wants to buy your product.

Aggressive objection-handling may set a tone that will turn off prospects from buying, even if you have overcome all the objections. Assuming you are in the position to attempt prospect closing, aggressive tactics can be perceived negatively by government prospects to the point of "turning them off." People do not like to feel manipulated, particularly those in government. Prospects may not agree to buy because their reasons are emotional or intangible. The salesperson may have won the battle but lost the war. A goose egg on the sales charts still amounts to zero no matter how craftily it was obtained.

Some of you may take a position that objection-handling and closing techniques are merely ways to surface prospect questions and pains--ultimately necessary for creating value in the customer's mind. We buy that to a point if it's truly your motivation.

There is nothing wrong with probing prospect pain points or preconceived notions and attempting to set the record straight where needed (**in fact, it's absolutely essential**). There is certainly nothing wrong with attempting to determine where the prospect falls within the buying process, or asking for the privilege of earning his business. Direct questions are fine, even appreciated.

However, when the process becomes more of a focal point than creating real value for customers, we draw the line. Objection handling and closing techniques are easily abused and should be avoided.

So back to our question: If customer manipulation through objection handling and closing techniques is not the right approach, what is the proper way to ensure deals are moved to finality? The answer lies in your ability to build customer value perceptions (through VP Selling) and your ability to practice "proactive constraint," otherwise known as "patience."

Build Value, Be Informed, then Be Patient

We've already introduced the key to winning--understanding and building a strong Value Portfolio story. If you are in the prospect's office before an RFP is issued, you certainly have the opportunity to learn pain points, explore solution options, respond to objections, and maybe even attempt to close the deal with a sole source contract. If not, you must, through established procurement processes and documents, uncover similar information—hopefully in a more effective manner than your competition.

Either way, you must develop a concise, compelling value story, and clearly communicate this in the proposal and the presentation. If you have done this to the best of your ability, then truthfully, the vast majority of your work is done. Often there will be no opportunity to trial close or make an assumptive close. Your ammunition is expended and you must simply WAIT. Patience is not something salespeople (or sales managers) are known for. After all, our job is to DO something--MAKE SOMETHING HAPPEN. You can certainly try to manipulate the process after proposals are submitted, but in the majority of cases it will get you reprimanded at best and thrown out of a deal at worst. So you wait.

It doesn't mean you stop selling. Here's what you must do instead of wasting your time on closing methods:

Be diligent in your efforts to uncover new opportunities and build a greater pipeline. Success in government sales is reliant on a large pool of opportunities. Some of them will close nicely. Others will fall out (often due to circumstances beyond your control). Keep doing the C.E.O. of Y.O.U. activities and keep multiple opportunities in play.

Keep close tabs on the decision process. If you have focused on relationship building, partners or coaches inside the organization should be able to provide helpful updates. Don't be afraid to ask. Let's repeat that. Do not be afraid to ask! Sometimes your questions will even help produce action. Again, ask.

Be ready to engage when you get the go-ahead. Your work isn't done in government selling just because you have received confirmation of a purchase. You will have to walk this thing through the remainder of the procurement process. Make sure you know the process and the players well. Ask again.

Do a post-mortem, if for some reason you do not get the deal. This will help you understand where gaps in your offering or sales approach existed. It's also a good idea to do a post-mortem when things went well and you won the deal. Positive reinforcement is often more powerful than negative experiences.

Realizing the limited role of objections and closing will enable you to more effectively focus on the really important aspects of selling instead of getting caught up in meaningless labels. Sales managers and salespeople wondering how to improve results should focus on the real issues—the ability to build relationships and create clear value—not an inability to close a prospect. Improvements will be found in looking further upstream in the selling process.

SAGE ADVICE

Pushing the Purchasing Process

Despite the frustrations we've experienced over the years, we have generally found that government buyers would like to move orders along just as quickly as anyone else. No one likes a full in-box. (Yes, there are still in-boxes on desks of government buyers.)

Some of the most professional and dedicated people we've dealt with are on the government buying side. You must believe this if you want to be successful. You won't move your orders along believing (and acting) otherwise.

A single individual somewhere along the bureaucratic process will not likely be able to completely derail your orders if you've done good work - even if you make them very, very mad. However, remember those full in-boxes? They are normally really, really full. Human nature would naturally make it tempting to place paperwork from an obnoxious jerk back in the in-box when there are plenty of other orders from us nice guys to process.

In fact, we've found lots of dividends in our belief that government procurement professionals really want to be helpful. We've not received any orders because of this, but we have been able to speed up the process by being nice and helpful.

[*Rick*] I once sped the process of receiving an order (and earning my commission to help pay for my daughter's wedding) by simply finding the right person, and nicely explaining why I was checking on the order – I had a wedding to pay for. Somewhere in the short conversation, they said, "Well, what do you know, the paperwork is in my in-box. Let me see if I can walk that along the process and see if we can help you out…and good luck with the wedding."

The order came in shortly afterwards, then the commission, just in time for the wedding bills. (Well, most of them.) No rules were violated. I didn't do anything other than nicely ask the right person for the status, and explain why I was asking.

The best way to be helpful is to make sure you've done all of the other things we've been writing about. Make sure you have good relationships, understand the pain you're trying to relieve, properly present a strong Value Portfolio, and follow the rules. And, as we have mentioned before, don't be afraid to ask questions.

A good question for a procurement person is, "Do you have everything you need from us?" Then, shut up and **listen**. First, they'll tell you if they need anything from you. Then, they'll likely tell you what will happen next. And, if you don't spill the beans at that point, simply ask, "What can we expect next"? Then, finally, "Is it OK if I check back with you?" Then, "When would be a good time?" Don't be surprised if they do not answer your email or phone call the next time you check back. Still, your polite and properly timed inquiry will at the least remind them check their in-box.

Seven Myths Take-Aways

- In government selling, you may not get the opportunity to close the sale.

- Multiple people are involved in buying make closing impossible.

- Aggressive objection-handling may turn off prospects.

- Build value, be informed, then be patient.

CHAPTER SEVEN

MYTH #7: Marketing and Sales are on the same page.

FACT #7: They're not even on the same planet.

A few years back, Dr. John Gray wrote a popular book on men-women relationships with the catchy title of <u>Men are From Mars, Women are From Venus</u>. The book delved into differences in the way men and women are "wired," how they approach relationships, ways in which they communicate, etc. The goal in reading the book is to understand and appreciate gender differences in order for relationships to improve and thrive.

A similar conclusion can be drawn with regards to differences in thinking, communication styles, and incentives between salespeople and marketing people. This can lead to significant frustration and conflict (the joke in marketing circles is salespeople are from Uranus).

Even if the conflict is not acute, companies may lose substantial leverage when sales and marketing are not aligned. If your company's sales and marketing functions are in lock-step, you are fortunate. Feel free to skip the next section. If yours is like most organizations, however, it's leaving money on the table due to ineffective collaboration.

What do we do about it? Let's examine why differences exist and what to do to get these critical groups on common ground.

Differences in Sales & Marketing

Strategic versus Tactical

The first area of conflict relates to differences in strategic versus tactical viewpoints. Allow me to let you in on a little secret. Marketing people think they know what's best for you and your company. You can't blame them, really. Just like men and women have been "socialized" to accept certain roles, responsibilities and interpretations of their environment, so have many marketing people been socialized to think they are the company's strategic organizational compass.

Much of this stems from the manner in which marketing people are educated and indoctrinated into their field. The vast majority of marketing principles are centered on consumer goods marketing. Procter & Gamble®, Coke® and Budweiser® are held up as the ultimate example of what "real" marketing is all about. Historically, brand managers within these companies are like mini-CEOs, making business decisions on factors ranging from pricing, advertising, promotions, product development and distribution. This is the model most frequently taught in universities and business schools across the globe.

In fact, on "Planet Marketing", direct sales is simply one option for consideration among a plethora of "distribution" channels (such as retail, direct mail, franchises, etc.). Marketing people often view sales as a subset of marketing, not the other way around.

The reality, however, is the business world as a whole is not like Procter & Gamble®. The brand management situation we've described does not fit a vast majority of companies—particularly those focused on selling to government. Many times, the marketing department is actually more of a "sales support" department, producing collateral material, advertisements, etc. that help salespeople sell. Marketing people, trained to be mini brand-CEOs, may balk at the idea of being "sales assistants" and push for greater strategic importance. Thus, conflict is born.

Customers versus Market Segments

Another key difference relates to the disparity in perspective between sales and marketing people. Sales people are trained and incentivized to focus on individual opportunities. They see the world on a granular, account-by-account basis (which is what they're supposed to do). When a customer asks for something the company doesn't offer (and heaven forbid a deal is lost because of it), the salesperson immediately perceives a wider market need, assuming many other prospects would want the same product or service feature.

Marketing people are trained to think in terms of broader market segments, positioning and niches. They rely heavily on market research studies that aggregate feedback from many different prospects and tend to reject individual account-level feedback as an insufficient sample. They also focus heavily (some say obsess) on the visual and tactile elements of a brand.

Conflict occurs when these two worlds collide. Salespeople think marketing folks just don't get it because they are not "in the trenches" hearing what prospects say. Marketing people think sales folks just don't get it because they only see in front of them that next commission check, and not the broader market needs or how to support the overall brand.

Compensation Incentives

A third difference between sales and marketing relates to incentives. Sales people are generally incentivized to land deals. A customer buys something and the salesperson earns a commission. Marketing people generally have a higher base salary (and less risk) and are incentivized on the overall growth in company revenue over the course of a year. This difference in compensation incentives lead to disparate levels of intensity, and potentially conflicting perspectives.

In truth, both ideologies have their place, and both are valuable to the organization. Unfortunately, these differing worldviews often leads to more negative consequences than positive results.

Aligning Sales & Marketing

How, as a government salesperson, do we help our organizations overcome this classic struggle? You may never turn a long history of disagreement into a corporate love fest. But, here are some key recommendations that just may improve things a bit.

Talk About It

Ironically, the two corporate functions with the most refined communications skills often converse the least. Honest, respectful dialogue needs to happen before things can improve.

If you are a sales VP or Manager, the ball is in your hands to create an opportunity for this dialogue. Don't wait for your counterpart in the marketing department to make the first move. Poorly aligned sales and marketing functions siphons dollars from you and your sales reps' pockets -- take responsibility for initiating the turn-around in the relationship yourself.

This is typically in the form of a heart-to-heart meeting between sales and marketing leaders. It may not immediately turn you into BFFs, but you might be surprised how much things improve. We first met when one of us was head of marketing, and the other was head of government sales. We worked hard to break down barriers between sales and marketing, which served our employer quite well, thank-you. What had been two forces moving separately became a more cohesive effort. Government revenues reached record highs and it became a much more fun place to work for both sales and marketing people.

Here are nine tips to help this go smoothly:

1. Take the initiative. Personally approach your marketing counterpart with the idea of the meeting. Tell him/her positive things are occurring, but you feel the need and opportunity to improve coordination. Ask to host a meeting to specifically discuss ways to improve the working relationship.

2. Keep the meeting small in number. Only a few key leaders should be involved in this type of discussion. Now is not the time to load up the meeting room with a hoard of complaining troops to illustrate a point. Do that, and you're just shooting yourself in the foot. It won't work. (Trust us, we've tried.)

3. Define the meeting. Make sure the goal of this meeting is clearly defined and focused around relationship improvement. It will not work (in fact it will backfire) if the marketing folks arrive expecting to provide a simple update on the latest direct mail campaign, only to be blindsided by deep questions surrounding why the overall working relationship is poor.

A clear meeting definition will give everyone time to think through issues and formulate ways to properly communicate sensitive information. Further, don't try to do too much in this meeting. Day-long sessions that encompass hours of tactical planning can be useful, but should be saved for another time. Spend an hour, maybe an hour-and-a-half in the first meeting.

4. Onsite or offsite? Decide if this meeting should be held on site or off. At times, it is better to get away from the office noise and interruptions in order to focus. Lunch may be a good idea.

5. Be productive and genuine. If your goal in this talk is really just to gripe and shift blame--don't bother setting up the meeting. You must commit to actually listening and understanding your marketing counterpart's perspective, focusing on concrete things that can be implemented to improve your relationship. This may include changes in some of your beliefs and attitudes.

6. Explore perceptions and feelings. It sounds mushy, we know, but often sources of conflict lie at very deep levels. Simply discussing "wish lists" of tactical items will usually not overcome core issues of fear and mistrust. Be ready to put feelings on the table.

7. Understand resource limitations. Be open to the fact that adding new projects to the mix drains limited time and money resources. Be prepared to trade off certain activities currently underway for new ones instead of simply adding more to the pile.

8. Bring in a facilitator. If the relationship is strained to the point where you doubt an honest, respectful exchange can occur, bring in a qualified outside moderator to help lead the discussion. Outside moderators can also be helpful when delving into deeper, hidden feelings and agendas. We both have facilitation training and skills, probably one of the reasons we were successful bridging gaps between sales and marketing.

9. Set expectations for a future check-point. Realize that one meeting will not suddenly erase years of misunderstanding and suspicion. Set a point in the future to reconvene and discuss how improvement efforts are evolving.

If you are a salesperson, and not a sales manager, don't think your influence is limited. First, make sure you are not part of the problem. Blaming the marketing department for your shortcomings, while popular, is not helpful and will be personally detrimental to you in the long run. Second, encourage your sales manager to build that communications bridge. You might be surprised how much influence you actually have over your boss. It may take several conversations and reminders, but eventually the message will get through that something must be done to improve the sales and marketing relationship. Third, foster your own connections. You must be C.E.O. of Y.O.U. Create your own conversations and relationships with people in marketing…even if informally. You will have a better perspective of their challenges, and they will be much more open to helping you when needed.

A Coordinated Attack on the Market

Achieving any significant military objective requires coordinated efforts of multiple branches of service. Prior to any ground troop offensive, air support will "soften" the targets through a barrage of firepower we've come to describe as "shock and awe." Even naval ships from many miles away may contribute to an inland battle through launching powerful long-range missiles. Once sufficiently pounded, ground troops can be deployed to overtake the target.

While political posturing and back-office conflicts between our country's various branches of service can be pronounced, these differences are placed aside once our brave men and women are activated. The objective becomes the primary focus of all parties.

This is a model of sales and marketing working together. As citizens, taxpayers, and family members of service men and women, we would be outraged knowing the Army refused to cooperate with the Air Force in the heat of battle. We would be appalled at the risk of each division deciding to "do their own thing" with no cross-branch coordination. We should be concerned when sales and marketing departments do not collaborate, operating in their own silos. It leaves money on the table in the form of lost sales, and it wastes precious resources.

In addition to a heart-to-heart meeting to get everyone moving in the same direction, sales and marketing must commit to regular and frequent interaction. Salespeople should attend marketing staff meetings regularly, and marketing people should be invited to sales meetings with frequency. Time must be spent understanding what is working and adjusting what is not. Where practical, invite a key marketing contact to accompany you on a sales call. This is a great way for marketing people to get in the trenches and hear firsthand what prospects are saying. You might even pick up some new perspectives yourself. Everyone will learn from the process, and bridges will be built. We guarantee it!

SAGE ADVICE

Winning Trade Show Strategies

Rick and I recently returned from working a government-focused trade show for a valued client. The show was a raving success, producing a sizable number of raw (but targeted) leads, and many strong prospects. Though booth traffic certainly had its ups and downs, it seemed we were able to stay engaged in meaningful conversations consistently throughout the four days of very long hours.

As the show was winding down, we naturally asked other exhibiting vendors within our vicinity what they thought of the show. We expected them to echo our feelings regarding its success. We were surprised at what we heard. Most exhibitors complained the hours were too long, the traffic was inadequate and the overall lead results were simply not that great.

As "glass half full" kind of guys, were we simply looking through the event with rose-colored glasses? Absolutely not! Our results were solid and recognized by vendors surrounding us (frustratingly so, I think). So why were we successful when others were not? Here are seven lessons we've learned over the years and applied here that can help make your next trade show experience productive and efficient.

1. Start with the Right Show

It sounds obvious enough, but it's astounding how much time, money and energy is wasted by companies conducting trade shows that don't really reflect their buyers. Many trade shows are essentially glorified fishing expeditions, attended in hopes of discovering some hidden pocket of lucrative customers. Rarely does this bear fruit. Surely exploring shows can be worthwhile, but you can do that by "walking a show" the first year instead of wasting a great deal of money and time on poorly targeted events. Make sure the shows you attend attract people who can really drive a deal.

2. Target Even More

Even for a well-targeted show, it's likely a large percentage of attendees will not be real prospects for you. Creating booth "buzz" is beneficial to some degree (we'll discuss this in a minute), but driving visits by legitimate, strong prospects is the ultimate goal. To address this, create a traffic driving campaign for the 40 to 50 people in your database you REALLY want to speak with at the show. Send them something that will get their attention and make them want to visit your booth. You may spend more per prospect this way, but you'll be driving the precise targets with whom you want to speak. What kinds of things will get their attention? Creative things--read on.

3. Get Creative

A little creativity goes a long way in generating booth traffic. Standard "trinket and trash" giveaways have their place but you may find a message-reinforcing campaign will yield greater results.

As an example, to capture prospects' attention, we sent our top 50 targets for this show a bright blue mailing tube (irresistible to opening). Open the top and Erector® set pieces fall out on their desk (a nostalgic construction toy that fit with the demographic of this show). A printed piece inside displayed an image of a helicopter made with an Erector set. The headline read "Making the Right Connections Can Really Help You Rise to the Occasion". The piece went on to describe how our system integrator client "makes the right connections" between disparate databases and systems in order to make the prospect's job more effective and efficient. It also invited them to drop by the booth and pick up their own Erector® set.

We successfully persuaded 40% of our highly targeted list to engage us in discussions with this campaign (many of the others were simply not in attendance). Further, we displayed several Erector® sets inside the booth. This generated nearly as many "drive by" discussions with people wondering about the relationship between a government-oriented technology company and toys. This was pure gold, as it gave us a chance to launch into our positioning pitch and start asking probing questions.

4. Lose the Table

If you are accustomed to sitting behind the big white table provided at many shows, you should rethink your approach. You're likely sending the wrong message to prospects. Tables are barriers between you and prospects. Sure they're nice places to stack literature, but you're not selling literature. You're selling solutions to problems. You cannot understand a prospect's problems until you get them talking. Tables are subtle but powerful deterrents to effective engagement.

Salespeople attending shows often assume they're stuck with whatever show management places in the booth prior to the show. Not so. Drag the table into the aisle at setup time and it will magically disappear before the show begins. If possible, rent a bar height chair and a small, round, bar-height table. Set these to the side so your booth is open and inviting. Though you should stand up during busy times, during slower times the bar height furniture will place you in a better position for engagement than slumping in some low-seated folding chair. Once a prospect approaches, stand up! Always stand when conversing.

5. Adopt a Consistent Lead Capture Process

This may range from those fancy badge scanners to simply making notes on business cards. Whatever the method, make sure it's consistent and practiced across all salespeople working the booth. There's nothing worse than lost leads or incoherent notes due to a sloppy lead capture process.

6. Leverage Vendor Events and Lunch

After standing in the booth for hours, it's tempting to want to slip away for a quiet lunch somewhere. However, if you are skipping the opportunity to have a meal with attendees, you are ignoring a great lead generation opportunity. Over the years, we've had innumerable productive conversations simply by plopping down beside some stranger and striking up a conversation with them.

7. Overall, Be Proactive

Too many times we see salespeople sitting back waiting for conversations to come to them. Remember why you came to the show in the first place (presumably not for the golf). Be proactive and assertive in talking with people and making connections. You don't have to be obnoxious to achieve this. Friendly, engaging questions will typically do the trick.

Chad Blackburn, one of Galain's sales partners, (he worked the booth with us at this show) is one of the best I've seen at this. He stands in the middle of the aisle ready to engage any moving target. A simple, "Hi there, where are you from?" typically stops people and allows him to initiate a conversation. Another favorite tactic of his is to bring a football to the show and toss it to people as they walk by. Hey, whatever works.

Trade shows can be frustrating and tiring. But they can also be a highly efficient means of prospecting and initiating a relationship. Keep these tips in mind for your next show, and maybe your experience will be even more profitable.

Seven Myths Take-Aways

- Ineffective collaboration between sales and marketing leaves money on the table.

- Get the two talking to each other and develop collaborative efforts to reach the same objectives.

- Take the initiative—it's your livelihood.

CHAPTER EIGHT

BONUS! MYTH #8

MYTH: If it is to be, it's up to me.

FACT: If it is to be, it's up to US.

We just love butt-kicking, independent spirit-types in this country, don't we?

James Dean, John Wayne, Rambo, Rocky, Jason Bourne, Bruce Willis in *Die Hard*, Sigourney Weaver in *Alien* …the list goes on of real or imagined heroes who, despite overwhelming odds, dig deep within themselves to overcome conflict and emerge victoriously.

These cultural images spill over into our professional lives, with many sales people envisioning themselves as lone knights, shielded with a polished presentation and armed with a silver-tongue, single-handedly slaying fire-breathing dragons with names like Prospect, Target, and Doomsayers, rescuing the company from the brink of doom.

It's no wonder sales and business development people feel this way. Such ideals are reinforced in sales meetings, books, movies, and seminars thousands of times each year. Sales pros are taught to pursue their work tasks, competitive adversaries, and sometimes fellow employees with all the finesse of a cock fight.

Truthfully, qualities of competitiveness and independence are highly desirable in sales people (we look for them ourselves in our own hiring). These traits can keep one going in times of failure, disappointment and outright defeat. They can provide motivation where money or title does not. People lacking a "more-than-their-fair-share-of-ego" don't usually last long in the trenches of the professional selling and business development battle.

However, in government sales these qualities must be tempered; there must be balance. Perhaps no other selling situation requires more teamwork than this. Government customer solutions often have complicated or custom requirements with a long-term delivery time frame. Government decision-makers need content, and lots of it. The procurement process itself is frequently complex, requiring the deployment of a wide spectrum of skills (all of which you may not possess). Ongoing service-level agreement stipulations and Legal Department paranoia (don't even get us started) may tie deals up in knots. These days, you may need some sort of channel partner to run the whole deal through, and there may even be considerable political implications and sensitivities surrounding the purchase that call for involvement from individuals far above your pay grade, as they say.

Government selling is no place for loners.

You probably already know this in your head. Now you have to feel it (and practice it). Stellar government sales people have learned to manage their egos and develop leadership competencies to bridge interactions with individuals both inside and outside the organization who contribute to their achievement.

Great. "But you don't know the Bozos I have to work with here," you protest.

Believe us, we do.

So, other than being aware of our dependence on others, what can we do? Let's look at some key groups critical to success and review our top strategies for leading collaboration efforts.

Key Group #1 - Partners (Channel and Otherwise)

In the world of government sales, few things are more important than good partners. Customer solutions are often highly complex, multi-faceted, with lots of moving parts. Depending on the project, single companies may not have the skills to pull off the complete project on their own (particularly true for small businesses). It is a useful strategy to become a subcontractor or take the lead as a "prime," and coordinate other sub-contractors.

Even if you *can* do all the work, you may not be on the proper purchasing vehicle to enable a sale to a given agency. Expending the effort and money to establish one's company on every possible vehicle is generally not feasible. As a result, bringing in a "pass-through" partner (basically paying a small percentage to another party in order to use their existing purchasing vehicle) can be an efficient and effective solution.

While this sounds easy enough, signing up a partner doesn't guarantee the cash register will ring. However there are two things that will make your life easier.

The Almighty "Communications"

The first key to working effectively with partners is diligent and constant communication. With any collaborative approach, the amount of continuous and meaningful communications has a profound impact on success. Think of your partners as members of the team and interact with them as you would any other internal department (maybe even better than other internal departments). Set regular meetings/phone conferences to discuss issues ranging from general market feedback to specific potential deals.

In the words of Ronald Reagan, "Trust, but verify." Poke and prod with questions and concerns. Even in the best of situations, misunderstandings can arise, jeopardizing the project and the customer relationship.

Do Your Part

Second, do not expect a partner to do your work. We have seen contractors trying to sell through partners expecting they will aggressively and successfully take the product to market, leaving nothing for the contractor to do but sit back and wait for money to roll in. We guess this may have happened somewhere some time, but it probably won't happen to you.

Channel partners represent other products and services. Unless moving your product is clearly the fastest and easiest way for partner sales reps to retire quota, their efforts will be spread across many different customers and market segments, dividing their attention (and leaving you wondering why more of your product isn't moving). You are the master of your destiny so don't let up. How do you keep the progress going?

First, give the same level of selling and marketing attention to your partners as you do your end customers. You must stay "top-of-mind" with them or interest will be diverted to the next "big thing" to come along. Second, give substantial attention and support to end-user sales efforts even when selling through a partner. No one can represent your product like you can. Where possible, engage the end customer in promoting your brand and solutions. Focus on the combined strengths between you and your partner, and then let the partner seal the deal.

Yes, maverick loners may make for entertaining movies, but they make for poor government salespeople. Polish up your collaboration and communication skills and you'll be much more successful over the long haul.

Key Group #2 - Senior Management

Play Nice with the "Bus Driver"

Who drives the bus in your organization? Obvious answers might be individuals such as the Chairman, CEO, President or COO. While these individuals may have the decision-making role, most senior executives have certain functional preferences—that is, leanings toward one part of the company over another when faced with options or dilemmas.

For example, companies with senior managers who "came up" through the technology side of the house are often product-centric ("Let's make cool stuff and see if we can sell it."). Companies with senior leaders who came out of the finance world often focus on financial ratios and banking relationships ("It doesn't matter what business we're in as long as we maintain our margins."). Some companies are marketing focused ("Before we commit resources, let's research what the market wants and then develop our business model."). And, some companies are sales-oriented ("Go sell whatever you can and find out what "sticks"; we'll figure out how to deliver it and what our business strategy will be from there.").

Determining the tendencies in your company gives you an idea of where to focus collaboration efforts in order to have maximum influence.

While senior management teams vary in personality, in general they view the world from a longer term, bigger picture perspective. This may conflict with the sales function's perspective which tends to be shorter-term, deal focused (mostly because they are incented by senior management to think this way).

To succeed in collaborating with this important group and get things done, learn to speak their language. Consider profitability and the need to hold to pricing. Realize they will want things like "business cases" and "ROI analyses" before pursuing new directions. Be honest with yourself and your management team about the *real* market potential represented by a single prospect.

Think responsibly about the organizational impact certain projects/sales would have. These are real issues that might come back to bite you down the road, in spite of a short term retirement of quota.

Also, develop and communicate your understanding of all the "levers" in business – not just sales revenue. Examples include cash flow, revenue recognition rules, cost drivers, operating margins, net margins, etc. Thinking from a broader senior management's perspective will demonstrate you are more than a one-dimensional player.

Key Group #3 - Product Management

While this role varies across industry sectors, generally there is a group of individuals in charge of determining product direction and futures—herein referred to as "product management."

In the technology world by example, product management is sometimes seen as the "S.P.T."[10] (that is the Sales Prevention Team). Salespeople bring the product management folks a great opportunity that will contribute to meeting the quarter's numbers, only to have it shot down as being too risky or outside of their technical comfort zones. Other industries have similar functions serving as filters between sales and product delivery. How do we collaborate with this group in order to move things forward?

One of the best strategies to improve working relations is to take them with you on sales calls. I realize how frightening a prospect this might be for some salespeople. Their greatest fear is realized in having in the room a deeply technical person, with no selling skills. Unbiased, non-sugar-coated, techno-babble answers to questions may, after all, deliver a fatal blow to the opportunity.

While clear parameters should be established by senior sales and product management leaders before attending an important prospect meeting, inviting the product manager to the party can

---

[10] Proper credit is given to Bill Carman for creation and generous use of this term.

prove beneficial. Plus, the prospective customer will likely be impressed. Some government buyers will insist on it.

Ultimately, great product management cannot be delivered effectively from inside the company's building. Customer needs must be heard, captured and analyzed from a true "market voice" perspective. If not, hearsay and rumors about what customers really need will rule. Sometimes this can work in your favor, sometimes not. Rarely does it work for the company as a whole. So, if the product manager needs to be in front of the customer, they might as well be there with you—the relationship gatekeeper—to monitor and moderate the interchange.

SAGE ADVICE

Rule You Can Break: The GSA Schedule

If you want to sell to the Federal Government, you have to be first on the General Services Administration (GSA) schedule…true or false?

Most would say "true." Most would be wrong.

Not that there's anything wrong with being on the GSA schedule. It's just not required to make government sales and win government contracts. This is a good thing. Getting listed on the GSA contract schedule is time-consuming and expensive.

Now, don't get us wrong. To be successful, you have to figure out how to make it as easy as possible for government customers to buy from you. Being on the GSA schedule certainly is one approach. But, there are other buying schedules that work just as well…some of them better, depending on what you're selling. (Some state and local governments use the federal GSA schedule.)

There is another route – partnering with someone who is already on the GSA schedule (or another appropriate contract). You won't get off scot-free. You'll likely pay the partner a portion of the sale and you will still need to follow the rules of the contract and the Federal Acquisition Regulation (FAR).

Yes, plan on getting on the right contracts, but don't even consider getting on GSA or other contracts as your sole federal contracting strategy. You simply cannot expect to make these arrangements and then see orders magically come in. You still have to make your value propositions to the right people at the right time. The contracts should be only one element of overall strategy.

Seven Myths Take-Aways

- Successful government selling requires collaboration with others.

- Channel partners, senior management and product management are prime targets for collaboration.

- Understand who really influences decisions in your organization and seek to focus collaboration efforts in the right place.

THE LAST WORD

Three Final Secrets to Winning

If you've worked your way through this book, you know we recommend you break a number of traditional "immutable" laws of sales. Hopefully, you now understand why old school sales techniques are just not effective in the government space.

Some of these recommendations require significant work and a full-blown change in perspective to implement. Others require only slight modifications to your existing approach. Whatever the case, we know the results are well worth the effort.

For a final bit of advice, we leave you with three overarching secrets for succeeding in government sales where others fail. These secrets support and extend virtually everything we've learned together in this book.

Secret #1 - Solve the problem. You might think this is obvious, but so many times we are guilty of pushing features and functions where we think we have a competitive advantage instead of presenting *real solutions* to real needs. In order to solve the problem, you must find ways to get prospects to open up and reveal their true pain. This means being there first (before the RFP is issued) whenever possible, and it means establishing good rapport and strong credibility. It also means discovering pain at different levels of the organization since the pain at one layer may not be the same as that of another. All of this culminates in a value portfolio that provides insight into what it will take to win a deal.

Once the problem is well understood, the solution offered must clearly and obviously provide a legitimate fix. "Smoke and mirrors" may win you the occasional deal, but real solutions create a long-term business. If you can't solve the problem, move on.

Secret #2 - Follow the rules. Rules and regulations are foundational elements of government markets. Contractors must be adept at following them. This doesn't mean a contractor can't have some degree of influence over the process. However, influence must come early in the process. Once RFP guidelines have been issued, for example, it might take an act of Congress to change them (literally). We have given you detailed information on how to build relationships and influence the process to your advantage.

Secret #3 - Make it easier than the next guy. "Ease" builds value in the government market (in all markets really). Even if your product solves the technical problem, and even if you've followed all the procurement rules, your solution still may not make the cut if another vendor demonstrates they are easier to work with. For example, do you have a contract "vehicle" they can use? End-users like to take requisitions to procurement people where a contract vehicle is already in place. Often procurement people are incentivized to use certain vehicles, rather than spending our tax paid money on the expensive RFP process.

These three concepts may seem elementary to some, but brilliant game plans will not win games with poor blocking and tackling. Keep these three fundamental secrets in mind and eradicate the selling myths holding you back and we believe you'll end up with the selling odds in your favor.

INDEX

96, 97, 98, 100, 108, 115, 116, 117, 118, 119, 120, 133, 134, 141, 142

prospects, 13, 15, 17, 19, 20, 21, 22, 23, 25, 27, 29, 32, 33, 34, 35, 36, 39, 40, 41, 45, 46, 47, 48, 49, 55, 66, 77, 79, 90, 93, 96, 100, 110, 115, 118, 123, 127, 131, 132, 133, 134, 147

psychology, 78

qualifications, 45

relationship, 12, 13, 14, 15, 16, 17, 18, 19, 20, 21, 22, 23, 24, 25, 26, 27, 28, 29, 30, 32, 33, 34, 35, 36, 37, 39, 40, 49, 120, 128, 129, 130, 134, 135, 140, 143

RFP, 6, 12, 13, 40, 62, 66, 77, 79, 82, 87, 89, 119, 147, 148

sales, 5, 6, 7, 8, 9, 10, 13, 14, 17, 19, 21, 22, 25, 26, 29, 31, 34, 35, 36, 40, 41, 42, 43, 45, 46, 47, 49, 51, 53, 54, 55, 60, 63, 65, 69, 74, 76, 77, 79, 91, 92, 93, 94, 95, 96, 99, 100, 101, 110, 115, 116, 117, 118, 119, 120, 125, 126, 127, 128, 130, 131, 135, 136, 137, 138, 139, 140, 141, 142, 144, 147, 154, 156

social media, 46, 52

solutions, 9, 27, 60, 75, 89, 90, 109, 134, 138, 139, 140, 147, 148

specifications, 12, 13, 69, 93

strategy, 13, 24, 26, 27, 28, 29, 36, 49, 63, 75, 77, 79, 112, 117, 139, 141, 144

trade show, 35, 48, 132

trust, 14, 15, 16, 17, 18, 19, 20, 21, 26, 29, 34, 36, 40, 111

value, 8, 12, 16, 18, 21, 22, 28, 48, 50, 52, 56, 68, 69, 76, 77, 78, 83, 85, 86, 87, 88, 90, 91, 96, 97, 100, 117, 118, 119, 120, 123, 144, 148

value portfolio, 73, 74, 76, 77, 79, 83, 86, 88, 90, 119, 122

values, 21, 22

vendors, 5, 53, 75, 92, 109, 132

white paper, 47, 50

Acknowledgments

Rick

Many thanks to my family, Kathy, Jessica, Shannon, Davis, Patrick and Jami. Who could ask for anything more? And, thanks to my Mom, Nita, a dedicated retired government servant, who's been teaching me how to sell to government all my life...although neither of us realized it at the time. She's taught, and continues to teach, me other cool stuff, too.

And here's to the memory of my Dad, Freddy, a true educator who taught me that teaching and selling are about listening, not talking.

Lorin

Thanks and love to Alecia, Victoria and Alexandra, the real joys in my life and true gifts from above. Thanks also to my parents, Benny and Gwen, for all their love and support over the years.

About the Authors

Rick Wimberly has served in sales leadership roles pioneering two of the most accepted public safety and government products of the last fifteen years. He has helped turn around several companies, and has been active in helping governments create programs producing real success. He knows problem-solving, and serves as a leader in an international organization that promotes creative problem solving.

Rick has deep success in increasing revenues in the government sector for critical communication technology. Customers include top agencies in federal, state, and local levels - particularly those involved in homeland security, public safety, and emergency management.

Rick serves as President and founder of Galain Solutions, Inc. and Government Selling Solutions (GSS).

Lorin Bristow has seventeen years of experience leading top organizations in sales and marketing operations, business development strategic planning, and market research. For much of the past decade, Bristow has helped drive sales growth for critical communications technology companies within the public safety, government, defense, and private enterprise sectors.

Prior to joining Galain Solutions, Inc., Bristow served as Vice President for the nation's largest provider of critical communications software. In this role, he managed marketing for two divisions and 40+ technology products.

He holds a Master of Business Administration degree from Vanderbilt University.

Lorin serves as Managing Partner with Galain Solutions, Inc. and Government Selling Solutions (GSS).

About Government Selling Solutions (GSS)

A Division of Galain Solutions, Inc.

With a proven track record of accomplishment in helping businesses win government contracts, GSS is uniquely qualified to help companies grow government business. Our principals have decades of experience and successes in marketing and business development to local, state and federal agencies.

We offer the following services:

- government sales training programs
- sales team assessments
- marketing and sales alignment
- market research services.

For more information or media inquiries, contact:

Government Selling Solutions
info@govsellingsolutions.com
www.govsellingsolutions.com

Made in the USA
Lexington, KY
09 January 2014